Worth to Dior

20th Century Fashion

from the collection of the National Gallery of Victoria

Robyn Healy

Photography by Helen Skuse

Sponsored by

LOUIS VUITTON
MALLETIER A PARIS

MAISON FONDÉE EN 1854

 Supported by

Published by the National Gallery of Victoria
180 St Kilda Road, Melbourne, Victoria, 3004

National Library of Australia Cataloguing-in-Publication entry:
National Gallery of Victoria.
  Worth to Dior.
  ISBN 0 7241 0165 9.
  1. National Gallery of Victoria - Exhibitions. 2. Costumes - History - 19th century - Exhibitions. 3. Costume - History - 20th century - Exhibitions. 4. Costume design - History - 19th century - Exhibitions. 5. Costume design - History - 20th century - Exhibitions. 6. Fashion - History - 19th century - Exhibitions. 7. Fashion - History - 20th century - Exhibitions. 8. Fashion and art - Exhibitions. 9. Costume - Victoria - Melbourne - Exhibitions. I. Title.
391.0090749451

Designer: Roger Saddington
Editor: Janet Bunny
Word processor: Judy Shelverton
Film reproduction: Colourbank
Printer: McPherson's Printing Group
Photographer: Helen Skuse

Cover illustrations:

DIOR, Paris est. 1947
Christian Dior, designer 1905–57
Detail from *Evening dress* autumn–winter 1956
silk tulle, metallic threads, plastic and metallic sequins
Purchased 1993   CT5-1993

Inset:
WORTH, Paris 1858–1954
Jean-Philippe Worth, designer 1853–1924
Detail of bodice from *Presentation gown* 1897
silk satin, silk chiffon, gold bullion thread, metallic sequins
Presented by Lady Nicholson
and her daughter 1951   1078A-4

Worth  to Dior

National Gallery of Victoria

Contents

Sponsor's Message

Louis Vuitton Australia is proud to be associated with the National Gallery of Victoria in bringing you this significant exhibition.

The time from 1890 to 1960 was an extraordinary time in France and particularly in Paris, including as it did the eras of the Belle Epoque, Haussman, the development of the Impressionists and the start of the first couture house — Worth.

The period also embraced two world wars and the development of Paris as the absolute fulcrum of fashion.

Louis Vuitton was there too; at the vanguard of design and innovation for wealthy and adventurous travellers. The road to fame for Louis Vuitton began when he was retained by the Empress Eugénie, wife of Napoleon III, and he designed, built and packed the trunks of the royal couple when they travelled.

Most of the clothing packed into the Empress' celebrated luggage came from the House of Worth, which, having attracted imperial patronage, quickly became the chief couturier for the entire French court.

Since then, the Louis Vuitton company has continued its close association with the grand couture houses of France.

We are pleased to continue our partnership with the National Gallery of Victoria, as it has always been our world-wide policy to support the cultural activities and so enrich the lives of the local communities in which we operate.

Worth to Dior is a particularly appropriate exhibition for Louis Vuitton Australia to sponsor and we are excited to be part of it.

Acknowledgements

I would like to thank the Director of the National Gallery of Victoria, James Mollison, for his encouragement and support both for this exhibition and for the Department of Costume and Textiles over the past three years.

Costume exhibitions are labour-intensive and require a large team of people to prepare garments for display. My thanks go to Catherine Millikan in particular for the conservation of the garments and for supervising our large band of volunteers, and to the volunteers themselves for their support and hard work: Margaret Tuohy, Wanda McPherson, Karen Quinlan, Esther Pierini, Marie Sweetman, Marina Holland, Christina Turner, Julie Ryder, Lisa Klepfisz and Palmina Santucci (VSO).

The support of the staff of the National Gallery of Victoria: Jacky Healy (Deputy Director Public Programs), Margot Capp (Executive Director, Business Council), Deborah Hart and Judy Williams (Business Council), Jenny Moloney (Publications), Jo Waite (Publications Designer), Judy Shelverton (Publications), Helen Skuse (Photography), Roger Saddington (Graphic Designer), Adam Worrall (Chief Designer, Exhibitions) and Daryl West-Moore (Designer, Exhibitions) is greatly appreciated, also the external support of Debbie Ward (Senior Textile Conservator National Gallery of Australia) and the contract conservators Carol Cains and Sue Ride-Gardboe.

This exhibition was made possible by the generous support of Louis Vuitton and encouragement by Julia King.

Robyn Healy
Curator Costume and Textiles

Director's Foreword

This catalogue and the exhibition it illustrates celebrate the National Gallery of Victoria's collection of couture costumes. The first textiles collected for this gallery in 1895 must have been seen at that time as useful illustrations of the union of art and technology. Today, textiles for the larger part are probably more dependent on technology than art, though there are cases when artists of consequence have been employed to design works for manufacture, and there are some exceptional artists who express themselves through the medium of fibre. Artists for whom I have the greatest respect are those few who, through their work in couture fashion, alter the way people dress for a season, a few years or a lifetime.

In their creations couturiers express themselves through colour, tone, texture, line and shape. Instead of work being made on a canvas, or from clay for display on a shelf or use on a table, their art is seen in movement on human bodies. The degree of innovation of the great couturiers and the excellence of their craft reflect the interests of artists who use different means of expression. The beauty of their fabrics, and the exquisite haberdashery designed for dressmaking use are the equivalent of beautiful paint or marvellous glazes. Individual designers have often found unique ways of combining these so that their signature is as easy to read as that of artists in other mediums.

We have a curious attitude to fashion in that we reject some things as too extreme when we first see them; rejection then is often followed by a wish by those who take an intense interest in fashion to wear the item. At the moment the smartest people begin to tire of the line we see it reflected in street wear after which, often for a period of many years, the style looks tired, the colours wrong: it looks old-fashioned. Then, with the passage of time, we are able to see the work as an art object, and we again enjoy the look, the line, the structure, the seams and details, and appreciate these as an expression of the artist's intent.

Clothes such as those illustrated here are extremely fragile; they are also at risk from exposure to too much light. Recently, curators in an Australian museum noted that a piece of poorly dyed orange silk faded to grey over a two-hour period. The clothes suffer stress even when left hanging on mannequins over a period of months. Clothes have to be prepared for exhibition by people with exceptional craft skills, working under instruction from textile conservators. Towards the conservation of items here, I have seen people spend tens of hours re-aligning sequins by flipping those that had turned over since they were first applied. The result is a spectacular return to the artist's intention for the garment, which after treatment no longer looks dazzlingly bright but has its original sleek look. I have watched as the silk lining which had come loose from a Chanel coat was re-sewn, using the finest silken thread through the still-visible old holes of original stitching. I also had brought to my attention the extraordinary cut of a Vionnet dress, constructed from small, finely sewn-together pieces of fabric.

I would like to congratulate Robyn Healy, the curator of *Worth to Dior*, for the concern she has for the history of fashion, and for her ability to convey her love for the items in this exhibition through their display and her accompanying text. She has been helped by all those who have volunteered their services to this collection, which, together, we present for your enjoyment.

James Mollison, AO
Director, National Gallery of Victoria

From Worth to the National Gallery of Victoria

Madam, who has recommended me to you? In order to be dressed by me you have to be introduced. I am an artist with the lone scale of a Delacroix. I compose and a toilette [dress] is just as good as a picture ... the women who come to me want to ask for my ideas, not to follow their own.

Charles Frederick Worth [1]

The period from 1858 to 1958 is significant in the development of the art of fashion design and of its powerful influence on directions and styles of dress in Western society. From Charles Frederick Worth, who dressed the Empress Eugénie and the royal courts of Europe, to Christian Dior, who revitalised the fashion industry by launching the radical 'New Look', this exhibition focuses on the work of the major designers of this period and on their ideas about shape, colour, structure and philosophies of fashion.

Styles in the first half of the nineteenth century changed slowly, often taking decades to evolve. Now it is difficult to comprehend how fashion could function without the powerful figurehead of a leading designer. However during the eighteenth and much of the nineteenth century royal and aristocratic wearers had initiated the fashions. New styles were instigated by royalty for sumptuous court occasions and the aristocracy had these copied by their private dressmakers. These fashions were illustrated in the fashion magazines which began to appear in the eighteenth century; women would study these expensive magazines and select a style. Fabric was purchased from the mercery and the garment made by a dressmaker. A milliner would trim the dress and make appropriate headwear; within this process original effects could occur but anonymously. Female dressmakers made clothes for women and men tailored for men.

VIONNET, Paris 1912–40
Madeleine Vionnet, designer 1876–1975
Detail from *Evening dress* c.1923
silk tulle, metallic threads, silk and metallic thread lamé
Purchased by The Art Foundation
of Victoria 1979   D20-1979

Charles Frederick Worth (1825–95) is considered the founder of modern fashion. He was responsible for establishing the first fashion house in Paris, specialising in the design and fabrication of female costume. Worth was the creator of original ideas; he developed new styles of clothing, made and crafted using the highest quality techniques and materials.

He saw his role as that of an artist, dictating to clients their clothing needs. He presented annual collections, from which his clients selected their clothes and foreign buyers and manufacturers could order patterns. Worth's organisation of dressmaking and its attendant skills and crafts became the basis of the system of haute couture fashion as we know it now.

At the highest level of the new profession a fashion designer was called a *couturier* or *couturière* and the art of original design, and of using the highest-quality skills in its execution, became known as *haute couture* (French for high dressmaking). Haute-couture clothing dominated fashion through the twentieth century and elevated fashion artists into famous and public figures.

Fashion is complex and blends art, industrial design and popular culture. Couture clothing is documented only in the wardrobes of the rich, but for most of the twentieth century high fashion has influenced the form of all fashionable female clothing. Dior wrote:

The dresses of this collection may be worn by only a few of the thousands of women who read and dream about them; but high fashion need not be directly accessible to everyone; it is only necessary that it should exist in the world for its influence to be felt. [2]

The publicity and media exposure given to high fashion spreads new styles and they are copied by manufacturers and home dressmakers world-wide. During their respective lifetimes, Worth, Dior and a relatively few others became household words synonymous with the best and latest in fashion design.

To look at a dress in a nostalgic way and reminisce about the days gone by gives us pleasure but more importantly, costumes should be viewed as the work of the designer and the maker, and judged by their form, construction, materials and technology, and for the intellectual trends that have led the designer to adorn or disfigure the body in this particular way. Costumes are now shown among other art works in galleries all over the world. Textiles and costume for a long time were the poor cousins of the decorative arts, a curiosity area. Items were often used as props to decorative arts displays and not judged on their own terms. It was not until the 1970s that fashionable dress became accepted as serious art collecting. The Costume Institute at the Metropolitan Museum of Art in New York was the first institution to arouse public interest in costume. The Costume Institute was formed in 1937 to collect costumes and accessories,

of all epochs and all peoples, which may serve industrialists, artists, art historians, craftsmen, and students of all kinds as well as stimulate in the general public an awareness of the importance of dress in the development of the human race and the relation of this field of design to the present and future impulses in American life. [3]

The success of this venture led to the Costume Institute being absorbed as a department of the Metropolitan Museum of Art on 11 December 1944. This major collection of costume is now seen in the context of other arts — providing a model for galleries world-wide. It is remarkable that the institute's holdings are acquired solely through donation. The collection received major exposure through the extravagant and wonderful displays of Diana Vreeland. Many shows aimed primarily at glamour and perhaps failed in their curatorial stance but they provided a well-needed boost of popular and financial support to the area. Another inspirational collection is the Department of Dress of the Victoria & Albert Museum, London, founded in 1844. In 1971 the late Sir Cecil Beaton, recognising that it failed to represent contemporary fashion, compiled an important collection of twentieth-century fashionable dress. He approached the best-dressed people of Europe and America to donate significant designer outfits to represent the art of fashion. Today this is among the few important collections of its kind in the world.

The National Gallery of Victoria has played a significant role in the development of a costume collection in Australia. In 1981, the first major exhibition of twentieth-century fashion in Australia was staged here. The exhibition *Fabulous Fashion 1907–1967* came from the Costume Institute of the Metropolitan Museum of Art, and gave Australians their first taste of fashion as art. The first group of textiles had entered the National Gallery of Victoria's collection in 1895, with the purchase of a small group of Indian block-printed textiles; however, it was not until 1948 that the first group of costumes came into the collection with the presentation by the Misses Butler of a group of nineteenth-century costumes.

In 1968 Marion Fletcher was appointed the first Assistant Curator of Costume and Textiles, followed in 1972 by Rowena Clarke who held that position until her retirement in 1990 when I was appointed. Costume and Textiles broke away from Decorative Arts in 1981 to become a separate department, which is about to be rehoused in a new purpose-built storage and display accommodation on the first floor, in the area previously used for the library.

Our collection covers an enormous area, representing Australian and international textiles and costumes from antiquity to the present day. The international fashion component focuses on the work of the most significant artists and makers and, in particular, on items that represent an important new style or technical innovation. Garments and accessories are accepted only in good condition and an unaltered state. It is necessary to restrict the number of garments entering the collection due to the enormous and continuing cost of storage, conservation and display. Unfortunately it is very difficult to balance a collection so that is represents properly both day and evening wear. Evening dresses predominate, as the initial expense and the special nature of the garments often inspire owners to keep them, while the less glamorous day wear is often worn out or discarded when it is no longer in fashion. Working retrospectively is difficult; we don't often have a choice in the availability of some items, size or colour.

The gallery's twentieth-century fashion collection has developed through acquisition and gift and includes the following significant purchases and generous donations.

In 1951 the gallery received the costume collection of the well-known British painter William Nicholson (1872–1949), father of the abstract painter Ben Nicholson, a gift of his wife, Lady Nicholson and

DESSES, Paris 1937–60

Jean Dessès, designer 1904–70

Detail from *Evening dress* c.1954

silk chiffon, silk taffeta

Presented by Mr John Kenny 1986

CT44-1986

daughter, Elizabeth Banks. Many of these costumes were used by Sir William as props for his paintings. Among the thirty-eight costumes is a group of five magnificent ball gowns designed by the French couturier Jean-Philippe Worth, which belonged to Sir William's wife's mother, Lady Phillips. Born Florence Ortlepp, she married Lionel Phillips on 22 August 1885 and lived in the Orange Free State of Africa. In 1898, during a stay in London, Lady Phillips wrote to Worth in Paris to arrange designs for a large wardrobe. Unfortunately, soon after the gowns were completed her husband died, and due to the conventions of the official period of mourning when only black could be worn, she was unable to wear the dresses until years later, 'the splendid gowns bought in Paris for celebratory occasions are now useless because of the prolonged period of mourning.'[4] The bodices were altered in the 1900s when she was able to again wear delicate pastels and rhinestones.

A most important addition was the Schofield collection, purchased in 1974 with the assistance of a special grant from the Government of Victoria. This impressive collection consists of over a thousand items representing Australian and international costumes dating from 1760 to 1949, formed by Anne Schofield of Sydney. She began collecting in 1964 and acquired the bulk of the material overseas, especially in England. This was added to in 1978 with a further purchase of one hundred items through The Art Foundation of Victoria. The strength of this collection is the impressive group of nineteenth-century costume and accessories representing every decade, with significant examples of court dressmakers from the

BECHOFF & DAVID, Paris

Day dress c.1910

cotton tulle, tape lace, silk embroidery floss, silk satin

Purchased 1974   D284-1977

turn of the century. There are some major examples of the work of early twentieth-century couturiers, including a rare dress from the small couture house Beer, and an unusual embroidered gown from Bechoff & David, where the great couturière Madeleine Vionnet once worked.

In 1979 the gallery purchased an extraordinary collection of couture garments from the wardrobe of Lady Curzon, born Grace Elvira Hinds, the daughter of J. Monroe Hinds, United States Ambassador to Brazil. Her first marriage was to Alfred Duggan, after whose death she married Lord Curzon as his second wife in 1917. Lord Curzon was the Viceroy of India from 1898 to 1905. He died in 1925. During the eight years of their marriage Lady Curzon entertained lavishly and was dressed by the leading couturiers of the time. In her memoirs she records an unspeakable incident that occurred when the Queen of Spain arrived for dinner at their London house.

OTTO LUCAS, London 1932–71

Otto Lucas, designer 1903–71

Black hat c.1947

felt, silk tulle

Presented by Thomas Harrison 1980

D233-1980

16

I realized with a flash of horrified recognition that the dress was replica of the one I was wearing myself. Both were made of white and silver brocade by Worth of Paris, and they were absolutely identical. [5]

Lady Curzon rushed upstairs and changed; later, when she confronted Worth about this, he said he thought it was safe to create two similar dresses because Lady Curzon would probably never visit Madrid! Lady Curzon died in 1958; her wardrobe reflects the extravagant creations typical of the post-First World War era and the radical changes in the shape and form of fashion. It includes nine costumes by the designers Paquin, Vionnet, Patou, Worth and Callot Soeurs.

The Lucas Archives were donated to the gallery in 1980 by Margaret Price. These give us an incredible insight into the local fashion scene. The Lucas company started in 1888 in Ballarat and became a world leader in the production of underwear. In 1934 it moved to Melbourne to manufacture women's fashions. Every year the firm would purchase *toiles* — copies of the original garments made in inexpensive material (*toiles de coton*) — from the leading Paris designers and use these as patterns to recreate garments for the Australian market. The collection of toiles from the 1950s and 1960s include examples by Nina Ricci and Pierre Cardin.

The gallery has also received many important additions through individual donations. After the exhibition *Balenciaga: Masterpieces of Fashion Design* in 1992 we were presented with a rare example of Balenciaga's early work, an 'infanta' dress from 1939. This was originally worn as a wedding dress by Janet Lovell Moran at her marriage to Harold James Carter in Melbourne on 24 May 1940 and was bought through Le Louvre of Collins Street. This magnificent dress was given to the gallery by Mrs Carter's grand-daughter, Sarah Bostock.

Our accessory collection was enriched by the fabulous group of hats assembled by the Melbourne milliner Thomas Harrison and through the generous donations of his clients in 1976 and 1977. The hats represent the entire spectrum of twentieth-century millinery design, including Harrison's own work from 1929 to 1976 and hats by influential French and English milliners such as Otto Lucas and Aage Tharrup.

During the Second World War the fashion for head scarves developed and they became popular accessories. The gallery in 1948 purchased a remarkable collection of eighteen silk scarves printed by the leading London firm Ascher Ltd and designed by major contemporary artists ranging from Henri Matisse to Henry Moore. Purchased from the Georges Gallery, Melbourne, this is possibly the second largest collection of its kind after that of the Victoria & Albert Museum in London.

Costume is a sensitive museum object. Permanent installations of textiles were once common practice, however exhibitions left in place for years caused irreparable damage to fabrics. Like works on paper, costume and textiles are difficult to preserve and require controlled display and storage conditions. It is necessary to restrict the amount of time they are exposed to light and consequently only a small amount of the collection can be displayed at any one time. The effects of light are cumulative and cause the fibres to weaken, dyes fade and lose their colour. All light causes damage, in particular, the UV rays, and therefore it is necessary to display costumes in a gallery space with no natural light, and to use UV filters

on all artificial light sources. The light source is controlled at a level of 50–70 lux (light measurement units) over a maximum period of three months. The brighter the display lighting, the more damage it causes to the costume; that is why the lighting is kept at low levels during an exhibition. After the exhibition is over, the costumes are stored in complete darkness and remain in storage for several years before they are displayed again.

Costume-display preparation is time-consuming and expensive. Fashion is designed to be worn and relies on a body shape to give it form. Costumes require custom-fitted supports to distribute their weight evenly. Static displays cause prolonged stress on garments and often additional undergarments are required to take the strain away from the original fabrics.

The conservation of textiles is not simply dry-cleaning and some mending. Treatment of the garments requires expert analysis and documentation before any work is undertaken. Each fabric and trim, and the technical processes involving finishes and dyes need to be identified, and original stitching distinguished from alterations. Stitching repairs involve working through the original stitch holes and not creating any new damage. The aim is to stabilise the item and prevent any further deterioration rather than make it look brand-new and alter its historical integrity. Conservation involves a variety of techniques including spot cleaning, washing, sewing and adhesive repairs, vacuum-cleaning with minute nozzles and ironing with a spatula. Garments cannot be treated like our own clothes and require trained specialists to undertake this detailed maintenance.

As we look at some of the major fashion designers from the end of the nineteenth century to 1958 through the collection of the National Gallery of Victoria, there are unfortunately some gaps and a few glaring omissions such as examples of the work of Paul Poiret and Elsa Schiaparelli. However this current exhibition, *Worth to Dior*, gives us a marvellous opportunity to show highlights of our fashion collection, and to plan for its future direction.

Notes

1   Cited in Anny Latour, *Kings of Fashion*, Coward-McCann, New York, 1958, p. 92.

2   *Dior by Dior*, trans Antonia Fraser, Weidenfeld and Nicholson, London, 1957, p. 217.

3   Jean L. Druesedow, 'In Style: Celebrating Fifty Years of the Costume Institute', *Metropolitan Museum of Art Bulletin*, New York, Fall 1987, p. 3.

4   Thelma Gutsche, *No Ordinary Woman: the Life & Times of Florence Phillips*, Howard Timmins, Cape Town, 1966, p. 250.

5   The Marchioness Curzon of Kedleston, *Reminiscences*, Hutchinson, London, 1955, p. 136.

The Birth of Fashion Design

In 1858, Charles Frederick Worth established the first couture house in Paris, specialising in dress design and fabrication, which dictated the styles of fashion to his clients. He designed the garment, selected the fabric, trims, colour, every minute detail, and invented the system which is the basis of modern fashion. Worth went on to direct the major fashion trends of the next four decades. His clothes were considered essential dress at all the courts of Europe. The richest women in society throughout the world felt they had to be dressed by Worth. He allowed a new fashion style a life of five years before making major changes. Among those he was instrumental in introducing were the crinoline, later the bustle, a dress without a waist seam, a court mantle that hung from the shoulders and many more.

WORTH, Paris 1858–1954

Charles Frederick Worth, designer 1825–95

Label for *Bodice* c.1870

gold ink stencilled on silk petersham ribbon

Presented by Miss M. Bostock 1963

521-5

WORTH, Paris 1858–1954

Jean-Philippe Worth, designer 1853–1924

Presentation gown 1897

Bodice and skirt

silk satin, silk chiffon, gold bullion thread, metallic sequins

Presented by Lady Nicholson

and her daughter 1951   1078A-4

It has always seemed ironic that the originator of France's great haute-couture industry was in fact an Englishman. Born on the 13 October 1826 in the small town of Bourne in Lincolnshire, Charles Frederick Worth was apprenticed at twelve to the London drapery firm of Swan and Edgar. He went to Paris in 1845 and secured a position at the leading mercers Gagelins et Opiguez. Here he met and married Marie Vernet and set up a small dressmaking department which was very successful. Gagelins exhibited some of the garments made here at the London Great Exhibition of 1851 and won the only gold medal awarded to France. In 1858 Worth started a dressmaking business with the Swede Otto Bobergh; they opened Worth et Bobergh at 7 rue de la Paix, with a staff of twenty seamstresses. Within two years Worth had secured the patronage of the Empress Eugénie, the wife of Emperor Napoleon III of France. Many people, especially in England, were outraged at the idea of men working in the intimate area of women's wardrobe, seeing ladies in a state of undress and actually fitting garments on them. Traditionally, since the seventeenth century female dressmakers had made women's garments and men as tailors made clothes for men.

The Worth family established the foundations of the couture industry and the organisation to steer and promote it. Worth was one of the first to create a collection in advance of each season to show to clients, from which they could select and have their dresses custom-made. Fashionable clients spent the spring and summer seasons in town and autumn and winter in the country. So the French couturiers showed their spring-summer collection in January and autumn-winter in July, to fit in with their clients social routine, a pattern that is still followed.

Throughout the twentieth century the system was refined. In 1911 the Chambre Syndicate de la Couture Parisienne was founded to represent Parisian couturiers. This organisation protects designers from piracy of styles, sets dates of openings for collections and determines the numbers of models to be presented. A dressmaker cannot become a couturier or couturière without membership of this group. To join today you must meet very strict criteria, including being a major fashion innovator, keeping a workroom in Paris and employing a minimum of twenty workers. A couture garment by rule must be entirely made to measure.

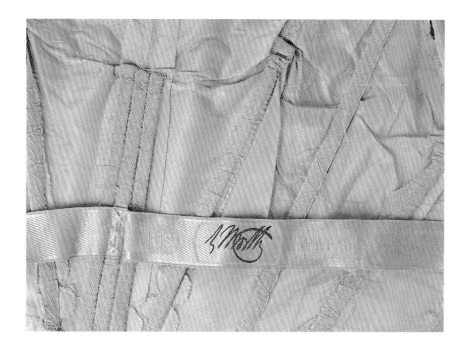

WORTH, Paris 1858–1954

Jean-Philippe Worth, designer 1853–1924

Label from *Presentation gown* 1897

silk petersham ribbon

Presented by Lady Nicholson

and her daughter 1951   1078A-4

After the style has been selected from the seasonal showing, the fabric is cut only after detailed measurements, countless fittings and often discussions of minor changes to the original design. The basic construction seams are sewn by machine, while the intricate finishing and detailing is completed by hand. In 1930 Jacques Worth was responsible for the formation of a school that is still active in training people in the skills of couture dressmaking . Each garment bears the designer's label and a unique model number ensuring the exclusivity of the design. Popular designs can be made as many as seventy times while some evening dresses are made only a few times.

A system evolved to protect designers from copyists by selling designs directly to manufacturers and retailers for mass production. Buyers pay an entrance fee to attend the collection, which contributes towards the payment of their order. A buyer purchasing from the parade pays more than a private client because the garment is to be used as a pattern. At a lower price toiles are available, which can be copied. It is also possible to buy a paper pattern with a sketch and fabric samples. By agreement the garment can only be reproduced a limited number of times, and the name of the designer must be placed on the label. Through this avenue the innovative designs of couture fashion reach a broader audience. Even today, every model created is registered in the couture house files, with a sketch, swatch of fabric, and photograph.

Worth et Bobergh was one of the first houses to attach its name to the garment; labels began to appear during the 1870s. The original label 'Worth et Bobergh' was stamped in gold on a inner waistband of petersham ribbon and bore the Imperial coat-of-arms from 1860 for ten years. In 1870 Bobergh retired and the house became Worth, and the label simply 'C. Worth'. The fashion label became a powerful symbol of status and prestige. In the nineteenth century usually only the maid saw these exclusive tags, although many a customer would proudly throw her coat or mantle onto a chair to reveal the mark of her famous fashion designer.

The period 1895–1914, known as the Belle Epoque in France and the Edwardian Age in England, was a time of excessive luxury and grandeur in architecture and the decorative arts. Worth's garments were detailed and fussy, flowing in the sinuous curves of Art Nouveau design in a reverse S shape created by a boned bodice, which pushed the bust forward while a slight bustle and train extended the trunk outwards in another curve.

After Charles Worth's death in 1895, his son Jean-Philippe became the chief designer. His work was equally flamboyant and stylish. One of his famous clients, the Australian opera singer Dame Nellie Melba, praised Worth in her memoirs, 'For making me realise how important it was to look as well as I sang ... some garments were dreams of beauty'. [1]

All three ball gowns from the Nicholson collection were made for Lady Florence Phillips in the same year and season. They give us an incredible insight into the extravagance of the wardrobes of the time and the design methods of Worth. With the house dressing every rich woman throughout the Western world, Worth produced thousands of gowns a year. This enormous output was only made possible by the

WORTH, Paris 1858–1954

Jean-Philippe Worth, designer 1853–1924

Skirt detail from *Presentation gown* 1897

silk satin, silk chiffon, gold bullion thread,

metallic sequins

Presented by Lady Nicholson

and her daughter 1951   1078A-4

23

WORTH, Paris 1858–1954
Jean-Philippe Worth, designer 1853–1924
Ball gown 1897
Bodice and skirt
silk satin, rhinestones, metallic thread
Presented by Lady Nicholson
and her daughter 1951   1078D-4

use of the Singer sewing machine for the long seams. Every stitch on garments before the 1850s was done by hand. The invention of the sewing machine revolutionised clothing production. A system of mass production was developed using a series of standard patterns with interchangeable parts. Worth would use the same basic shape for each garment but change the base fabric or trimmings to create a unique dress. Lady Phillips' 1898 wardrobe included a presentation gown, an essential item for those who were to be formally presented to royalty. (By 1897 it was possible to write or telephone orders and receive a mail order garment if it was not convenient to visit one of the firm's branches.) As we know, due to the death of her husband Lady Phillips could not wear her new dresses for several years and our magnificent *Presentation gown* (1897) was possibly worn by her at the coronation of Edward VII in 1901. The bodice was slightly altered to accommodate her larger size and the edge of the boned bodice tucked under; this has since been restored to its original shape.

The gown is of cream duchess satin comprising a separate bodice and skirt, and is ornately decorated with finely executed applied work. The bodice and skirt border feature an elaborate design of wheat sheaves, decorative festoons and tassels dripping with jewels, executed in gold bullion thread, metallic sequins, diamante and appliqué work in tan and green chiffon. The bodice is reinforced with whale bone encased in the lining to hold the bodice in a round curved shape. Whale bone, cut into thin flat strips, came from the plates or blades of the roof of the whale's mouth. This material was light and very flexible though the boned clothes were not necessarily comfortable to wear. The whale bone was difficult to prepare and very expensive, and was used until the first decade of the twentieth century. The bodice is fastened with hooks and eyes.

The House of Worth created countless new dressmaking techniques, including the gored skirt. Previously the rectangular panels of the skirt were fitted at the waist by gathering, Worth created panels that were wide at the bottom and narrow at the top and could be neatly joined at the waist. This perfect shape and smoothness of the skirt without complicated seaming or darting was a feature of the house.

The *Ball gown* (c.1897) displays the intricate embroideries which were an important feature of the Worth style. The white satin bodice and skirt are encrusted with rhinestones, silver metallic thread, glass beads and tiny silver metal sequins forming meandering tendrils of flowers and leaves. These intricate embroideries were executed by hand and worked on the fabric pieces before the final seams were done to allow for an unbroken sweep of embroidery.

Cleaning these magnificent ball gowns was difficult and was the responsibility of the maid, who would use various spot-cleaning methods including rubbing the cloth with substances like pipeclay or mason's dirt, and spirits. It was not until the second half of the twentieth century that the care and maintenance of garments became a design criterion and that the materials and cleaning instructions were marked on the label.

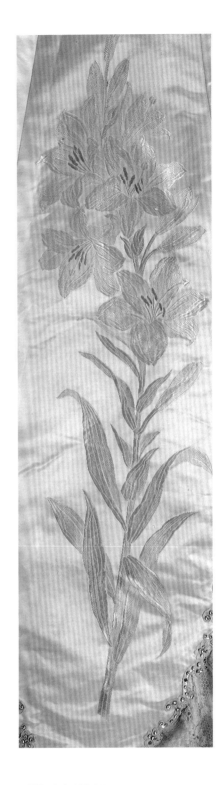

WORTH, Paris 1858–1954

Jean-Philippe Worth, designer 1853–1924

Skirt detail from *'Christmas lily' ball gown* 1897

silk satin, silk chiffon, diamante

Presented by Lady Nicholson

and her daughter 1951   1078B-4

RUSSELL & ALLEN, London est. 1880s

Ball gown c.1890

Bodice and skirt

silk satin, silk velvet, imitation jewels,

peacock feathers

Purchased 1974   D177-1974

Textiles were an important part of the design at the house. Worth worked closely with the silk-textile manufacturers of Lyons to make fabrics exclusively for his designs; the results were breathtaking. The *'Christmas lily' ball gown* (c.1897) features one of these individual designs, the cream satin fabric is woven with a large pattern of Christmas lilies in pale pinks, yellows and greens; each motif is eighty-two centimetres long. Illustrations of Worth clothes in the leading fashion magazines of the time were widely copied by smaller dressmaking establishments and home dressmakers.

Paris has been a centre of fashion for centuries, however there were also significant fashion establishments across the Channel in London. After the disturbances caused by the fall of the Second Empire in 1870 it was difficult for wealthy Englishwomen to travel to Paris for new clothes and many chose to support their local talent,while others felt it was vulgar to be dressed from Paris. Exclusive professional dressmakers in England were known as court dressmakers, this title does not imply that they made clothing specifically for royalty, rather they specialised in making presentation gowns. Their premises were quite large, consisting of a salon, fitting rooms, and workrooms. Presentation gowns were required for debutantes who were presented at court. The garments had to be designed according to rules set down by the Lord Chamberlain's office. The evening-style dresses had a court train suspended from

the shoulders, the length of the train was restricted to not more than eighteen inches (about forty-six centimetres) from the wearer's heel. The gown could be of any colour but almost always was worn with gloves and a headpiece consisting of a veil and three vertical feathers.

Russell & Allen, one of the leading court-dressmaking establishments, used a label combining English and French languages that boasted 'Robes de Bal' from 'Londre', giving them a continental air. The *Ball gown* (c.1890) combines a separate bodice and skirt of pale yellow satin and olive-green velvet. These bold colour combinations were common, and yellow was very popular during the 1890s, especially with violent contrasts such as scarlet. The yellow satin bodice has a V-shaped neckline and short sleeves with an elaborate drapery of olive-green velvet swathed across the left side in the manner of large sash. The drapery is decorated overall with fine embroidery in a Persian-inspired design of paisley and peacock-feather motifs, couched in gold metallic thread and accentuated with glass beads simulating semi-precious stones such as opals and moonstones. The right side of the bodice is dotted with coloured rhinestones ranging from pale blue to pink. The short sleeves are slightly gathered at the shoulders and have velvet cuffs decorated in a similar manner to the bodice front.

The back of the bodice has a higher neckline and features sixteen pairs of embroidered eyelets for lacing and fastening the garment. Below the waist are four vents outlined in large coloured rhinestones encircled by gold metallic braid. The bodice is boned and the label attached to the inner waistband. The double skirt with a green velvet train is richly embroidered and trimmed with peacock feathers.

The house of Redfern grew from very humble beginnings to become one of the leading and influential fashion houses of its day. John Redfern of the Isle of Wight began his business as a draper and by 1871 had expanded it to include a tailoring department, catering for the rich and fashionable set who came to Cowes for the yachting regatta. He established a reputation as a maker of ladies' yachting outfits, and spread into other areas associated with outdoor and sporting activities such as shooting, fishing and driving. The production of 'tailor-made' clothes for women was new.

In 1879 he opened a branch in London, still specialising in ladies' tailor-made costumes for outdoor and sporting activities and enlarged its range to include fashionable dress. Redfern received the ultimate

REDFERN, Paris est. 1881

Evening dress c.1895

silk satin, silk chiffon, rep silk, jet beads

Purchased 1974   D187-1974

recognition of success in 1888 when he was appointed the chief dressmaker to Queen Victoria and also the Princess of Wales, later Queen Alexandra. In 1881 Redfern sent Charles Poynter to France to establish a Parisian branch and later branches were opened in New York and Chicago.

The *Evening dress* (c.1895) of cream satin and black chiffon trimmed with jet beads was probably worn by a young widow during her half-mourning period, indicated by the use of black and white and the restrained decoration. The separate bodice with a low V décolletage is covered with black chiffon, the large balloon sleeves of cream satin are patterned with embroidered jet beads in a *fleur de lys* design. The inside of the bodice has eleven covered bones and is laced down the back. It has a tiny waist of twenty-one inches (about fifty-four centimetres).

The sleeves can be cleverly folded so that a long-sleeved bolero (fitted jacket) can be worn over the top. The jacket in black moire taffeta has white lapels sewn with jet beads in a floral pattern. The skirt, consisting of six gores, has no gathers at the front. This keeps the front flat and ensures the fullness keeps to the back of the skirt, which is shaped to sit on the hips and then flares with a slight train at the back. The hem is decorated with a border of jet beads in a *fleur de lys* pattern.

There were also a number of high-quality but smaller and cheaper dressmaking establishments that could produce the very latest fashion trends. The *Day dress* (c.1901) in sage-green damask by Mrs Eliot Vaughan of 71 Baker Street, London has a high collar and yoke of open-work lace with machine-embroidered mauve-coloured roses, highlighted in gold metallic thread. The inside of the bodice is a fine example of the high-quality workmanship of these establishments. The interior is lined with a cotton sateen printed with a small geometric pattern. The seams are machine-sewn and the raw edges oversewn by hand to neaten them. The label is printed in gold on the petersham waistband. The inner waistband or waist 'stay' is fastened with hooks and eyes and secures the garment, preventing it from moving.

It was essential to wear a corset to maintain the fashionable monobosom, which produced the curious S-shaped profile. The corset was a very complicated garment made from as many as fifteen curved pieces of fabric on each side plus the gussets, all beautifully pieced together and encased with ribs of whalebone and steel.1904 and 1905 were the peak years of the S shape and then dresses began to straighten up. The French *'Lingerie' dress* (c.1909) with a choker collar, puffed short sleeves, and a bodice pouched in front over the taffeta cummerbund, is unboned but would still have been worn with a corset. The skirt has four layers: a base layer of silk taffeta, then one of silk chiffon, and then a decorative tier combining lace, tulle and muslin with applied tufted braid in garlands of flowers, and a scroll design of ribbon insertions and tassels. It finishes with a split half-skirt in Valenciennes lace featuring a clover pattern. The skirt has a slight train edged with a lace flounce. This type of dress was worn in summer and was made from an assemblage of antique and modern lace and embroideries.

The *Day dress* by Bechoff & David (c.1910) is an elaborately constructed silhouette. The looser fitting bodice with no built-in boning and the higher Directoire waistline show the straighter shape, although the features of the high boned collar and trained skirt remain. The dress would also have been worn over a lightly boned foundation garment and princess petticoat. An unusual feature of this dress is a short overtunic of tape lace with hand-worked fillings. The dress is fastened from the back with twenty-four metal hooks and embroidered eyes, and would require the careful hand of a maid. The white cotton tulle skirt is richly hand-embroiderered with dandelion flowers and foliage in grey and ivory silk floss and the hem trimmed in pale pink satin ribbon.

The small couture house of Beer on the Place Vendome in Paris opened in 1905 and was a very fashionable house until the First World War. The simple lines of the *Day dress* (c.1912), created from white muslin with the bodice part-lined in black chiffon and trimmed on the bodice and hemline with guipure and filet lace, herald the new design directions. The dress, with the new raised Directoire waistline, has no bodice boning and no train, giving it a straight line.

Note

1   Nellie Melba, *Melodies and Memories*, Nelson, Adelaide, 1980 edition, p. 104.

FRANCE 20th century

Designer unknown

Detail from *'Lingerie' dress* c.1909

silk net, cotton lawn, tufted braid, silk ribbon

Purchased 1974   D212-1974

REDFERN, Paris est 1881

Label for *Evening dress* c.1895

woven silk

Purchased 1974   D187-1974

MRS ELIOT VAUGHAN, London

Label for *Day dress* c.1901

gold ink stencilled on silk petersham ribbon

Purchased 1974   D198-1974

BECHOFF & DAVID, Paris

Label for *Day dress* c.1910

silk satin, silk thread, machine embroidery,

inscribed and stamped in ink

Purchased 1974   D284-1977

BEER, Paris est. 1905

Label for *Day dress* c.1912

woven silk, silk thread,

machine embroidery, inscribed in ink

Purchased 1974   D218-1974

RUSSELL & ALLEN, London est. 1880s

Label for *Ball gown* c.1890

gold ink stencilled on silk petersham ribbon

Purchased 1974   D177-1974

Alternative Dress

From the middle of the nineteenth century there was a trend towards the rejection of fashionable dress with uncomfortable bones,crinolines and bustles. The artists and followers of the Pre-Raphaelite movement advocated simple flowing dresses based on classical styles. The Pre-Raphaelite artists did not depict contemporary clothing in their paintings; the embroidered panel *Poesis* (c.1880), designed by Edward Burne-Jones and William Morris, shows the female form of Poetry seated on a throne surrounded by the Muses and Sages. The uncorsetted figures are wearing classical dress, simple tunic-like garments accentuating the natural shape of the wearer's body , unaffected by the moral constraints of the day.

The International Health Exhibition of 1884 held in London devoted a large section to hygenic clothing, alerting people to the problems associated with certain types of restrictive fashionable dress, and displayed a selection of alternative styles. Many were simply variations of contemporary fashion.

The English firm of Liberty however, largely rejected current dress styles and produced garments which were inspired by historical modes or other cultures. Founded in 1875 by Arthur Lasenby Liberty in Regent Street, London the business started as an import shop offering exotic antique oriental wares. Liberty was also always associated with fine-quality fabrics, selling imported materials and commissioning leading decorative artists such as William Morris and Arthur Silver to design for the firm. A clothing department was established in 1884 under the direction of E. W. Goodwin, to promote Liberty's soft draping fabrics and to encourage their use by dressmakers. It was initially advertised as a new school of dressmaking, to challenge the fashionable dress of Paris and lead women to wear hygenic and progressive clothing. There were two basic styles: 'Novelties for the new season', based on current

THE ROYAL SCHOOL OF ART NEEDLEWORK, London est. 1872

William Morris, designer 1834–96 **Edward Burne-Jones, designer** 1833–98

Poesis, panel c.1880 wool, cotton

Purchased through The Art Foundation of Victoria with the assistance of Miss F. MacD. Anderson

Founder Benefactor and Mrs E.E.O. Lumsden Founder Benefactor 1992   CT11992

LIBERTY, London est. 1875

'Burnous' evening cloak c.1895

silk satin, silk embroidery thread

Purchased 1977   D85-1977

styles and featuring hand embroidery and smocking, or 'Costumes never out of fashion' inspired from classical and historical modes. One of the most popular models was the tea gown, a loose, flowing, indoor dress which was worn uncorsetted and with few undergarments.

Another influential garment promoted by Liberty was the burnous, an adaption from a type of Middle-Eastern wrap, originally worn by the Moors and Arabs in Northern Africa as a travelling cape. This featured a square hood with tassels at the corner. The Liberty burnous was worn as an evening wrap. The *'Burnous' evening cloak* (c.1895) of gold satin is edged along the front with a hand-embroidered floral border in muted tones of pink, green shades, blue and beige outlined in black silk, and has two large self-covered buttons embroidered with florets, fastened with loops of crocheted silk thread. The end of the rectangle of fabric forms a hood sewn with a silk tassel. Liberty opened a branch in Paris in 1894, but these alternative fashions caused no major changes in this city, as French women, although admiring them from a distance, remained loyal to the great houses of haute couture.

Throughout the twentieth century the unconventional dresses of the self-taught dress designer Mariano Fortuny have been admired and are still occasionally worn today. Born in 1871 in Granada, Spain into a wealthy artistic family, Fortuny began his career as a painter, delving into advanced art forms, and also followed scientific pursuits.

Fortuny was inspired by classical dress as we know it from antique sculpture, the dance costumes of Isadora Duncan and the reform movements, to create a form of dress that was comfortable to wear and beautiful, a perfect garment never going out of style. Lady Diana Cooper describes these dresses in her memoirs as if they were created by magic and belonged to no definite age

'Timeless dresses of pure thin silk cut severely straight from shoulder to toe and kept wrung like a skein of wool. In every crude and subtle colour, they clung like mermaids scales'. [1]

Fortuny had a varied education and was a great inventor, in particular delving into the area of theatrical lighting and stage craft. His approach to dress design was unorthodox. He regarded his new dress as an invention, registering it in Paris in 1909. Describing the tea gown of pleated silk as a garment 'derived from the classical robe, but its design is so shaped and arranged that it can be worn and adjusted with ease and comfort' [2], he named it the 'Delphos' after the famous bronze statue of the Charioteer (470 BC) found at Delphi and now kept in the museum there. He wears a chiton, a simple garment hanging in loose folds tied with a belt at the waist. The first Delphos gowns were made around 1906.

FORTUNY, Venice est. 1904
Mariano Fortuny, designer
1871–1949
Detail from *'Delphos' tea gown* c.1920
pongee silk, Venetian-glass beads
Purchased 1977   D82-1977

FORTUNY, Venice est. 1904

Mariano Fortuny, designer

1871–1949

'Delphos' tea gown and belt c.1910

pongee silk, metallic paint, Venetian-glass beads

Purchased 1986   CT2-1986

The construction of these garments was ingeniously simple. Four pieces of pre-pleated silk were hand-sewn together in a cylindrical shape. The neckline and sleeves were threaded with a drawstring and weighted with tiny Venetian-glass beads. The pleated silk was crimped horizontally and hand-dyed in an extraordinary palette of shimmering colours. The Delphos dress, basically a full-length gown in pleated silk, came in many variants. Our bright pink sleeveless *'Delphos' tea gown* (c.1910) is made from the usual four panels of pre-pleated hand-sewn silk. It is worn to cover the feet and hangs about ten centimetres onto the floor. Fortuny preferred the gown to spread a little at the feet as the wearer moved. It can be worn with a simple stencilled belt.

One of intriguing aspects of these gowns is how the pleats were created. All we know is the pleating was carried out when the material was wet and heat was applied at some stage to set it. It must have been a labour-intensive process, since all the folds are different and irregular. The pleated silk was next placed between a series of tubes that could be heated from within to undulate the fabric horizontally.

A range of velvet over-garments was designed to be worn with the Delphos, including jackets, coats and capes. The three-quarter length *Jacket* (c.1910) with long sleeves of dark green velvet is stencilled in a silver metallic pigment with a pattern of griffin-like creatures inspired by Italian Renaissance velvets. Fortuny liked his textiles to look antique and would intentionally create crinkled or flaky effects. The jacket is lined in a bright pink silk and features the beautiful Fortuny label, a circle of rep silk hand-stencilled and hand-sewn to the lining.

The pale pink *Double 'Delphos' tea gown* (c.1920) has short batwing sleeves with an attached short tunic hanging in points at the sides. The size of the dress is adjusted by the drawstring through the neckline and sleeves. The edge of the sleeves and tunic also have Venetian-glass beads, to weight the silk and control the shape of the garment. The dress is made from five hand-sewn panels of pre-pleated silk. Delphos dresses are difficult to date, however the early models are made from four lengths of silk and later a fifth section was added to fit larger sizes. The dress was worn with few undergarments. It was considered risqué and was at first worn at home as a tea gown. In the 1920s and the 1930s as the dress codes relaxed, the garments were more widely seen and were worn out to theatre and restaurants.

Fortuny produced Delphos dresses and velvet over-garments for his entire design career until 1949. He marketed his own garments and textiles, first in Venice and later in London, Paris and New York. His work was promoted by word of mouth and he rarely advertised in fashion magazines. His garments took on cult status with influential admirers such as Marcel Proust, Isadora Duncan, Peggy Guggenheim and, more recently, Tina Chow.

N o t e s

1   Diana Cooper, *The Rainbow Comes and Goes*, Century Classics, London 1986, p. 61.

2   Guillermo de Osma, *Mariano Fortuny: His Life and Work*, Aurum Press, London, 1930.

FORTUNY, Venice est. 1904

Mariano Fortuny, designer

1871–1949

Detail from *Jacket* c.1910

silk velvet, metallic paint

Purchased 1986   CT2-1986

FORTUNY, Venice est. 1904

Mariano Fortuny, designer

1871–1949

Label for *Jacket* c.1910

gold metallic paint, stencilled on rep silk

Purchased 1986   CT2-1986

PAQUIN, Paris 1891–1956
Madame Paquin, designer Died 1936
Label for *Evening dress* c.1920
woven silk, silk thread, machine
embroidery, inscribed in ink
Purchased by The Art Foundation
of Victoria 1979 D18-1979

JEAN PATOU, Paris est. 1919
Jean Patou, designer 1887–1936
Label for *Evening dress* c.1920
silk satin, silk thread, machine embroidery
Purchased by The Art Foundation
of Victoria 1979 D19-1979

VIONNET, Paris 1912–40
Madeleine Vionnet, designer 1876–1975
Label for *underbodice* c.1927
silk satin, hand embroidered
with signature and ink thumb print
Purchased by The Art Foundation
of Victoria 1979 D23B-1979

LANVIN, Paris est. 1909
Jeanne Lanvin, designer 1867–1946
Label for *Evening jacket* summer 1929
silk crêpe, silk georgette, glass beads
Presented by Mrs A. Wilson 1982
CT12A-1982

Function and Form

The early twentieth century saw major changes occurring in the style and function of fashionable dress. These stressed freedom of movement, less cumbersome undergarments and new shapes for more active lifestyles. The French couturier Paul Poiret represents the new spirit in fashion. He rejected the restrictive clothing of the past, promoting looser clothes worn without corsets in wild colours and exotic fabrics. Training under the traditionalists Doucet and Worth, Poiret formed his own house in 1904 to follow his startling ideas. He gave women imaginative garments from harem trousers to hobble skirts and turbans with aigrettes (sprays of feathers). He legitimised radical fashions akin to designs for the performing arts. In 1908, the arrival in Paris of the Ballets Russes de Serge Diaghilev had a major impact on

PAQUIN, Paris 1891–1956

Madame Paquin, designer Died 1936

Evening dress c.1920 and *Opera coat* spring–summer 1920

silk satin, metallic lace, imitation jewels, silk and metallic

thread lamé, gelatin sequins

Purchased by The Art Foundation

of Victoria 1979   D17/18-1979

fashion. Loose, flowing garments that accentuated the natural shape of bodies and exotic styles incorporating vibrant contrasting colours changed the look of fashion.

Oriental styling was a major feature in the work of Madame Paquin, the first important female couturière. The couture house Paquin opened in 1891 on the fashionable rue de la Paix in Paris. Its founder Madame Joseph Paquin, born Jeanne Becker, had trained at Maison Rouff. She used clever new marketing techniques, taking her mannequins to the races or opera, often in identical outfits, to advertise and promote her latest designs. Paquin was the first couture house to open branches outside Paris, beginning in 1898 with a London branch followed by shops in Buenos Aires, Madrid and a fur shop in New York.

Renowned for her opulent, luxurious clothes and supple fur garments. Paquin also experimented with the cut of clothes, to achieve a narrow silhouette which allowed for ease of movement. This required a blend of clever drapery and tailoring.

The *Opera coat* (spring-summer 1920) in a pale gold lamé cocoon-shape reflects oriental styling with its sloping shoulders and kimono-like sleeves. The lamé is embellished with random roundels of stylised roses and leaves, delicately formed by pale opalescent sequins and clear glass beads coloured from within by a roll of silver foil or coral paper. The coat is highlighted with borders of gold metallic lace and lined in a dull pink silk velvet. The rose is the symbol of the house and features on the woven label that is inscribed with the client's name, Madame Curzon.

Paquin's *Evening dress* (c.1920) of white silk satin in a simple tubular line is offset by diamante shoulder straps and a hip border . The gold metallic lace overskirt edged with rhinestones features a delicate design of reindeer.

An incredible range of luxurious fabrics was developed with new and innovative optical and textural qualities. Evening garments of the 1920s feature these marvellous materials. Jean Patou, one of the leading Parisian couturiers of the 1920s, created clothes for active women in simple, functional lines; his clothes epitomise 'chic'. Born in Normandy in 1888, he opened his fashion establishment Maison Parry in 1912, closing in 1914 when he joined the French army. After the First World War, he reopened his house in 1919 under his own name. During the 1920s Patou produced exciting and modern clothes inspired by the Art Deco movement, using dynamic colours and magnificent fabrics in cubist shapes. From 1914 until his death in 1936 he was a leading innovator.

The *Evening dress* (c.1920), a vertical line in fuschia and gold lamé, has a fabulous pattern of galloping horses. The sleeveless dress with a bateau neckline, straight from one shoulder to the other, has a dropped waistline down to the hips, accentuated on one side with a rosette and on the other with a streamer trimmed with beaded fringing. This wild fuschia shade is probably a signature colour. Patou had his fabrics created to order and colours dyed to his instructions, producing unique and very expensive materials that were impossible to copy. The new textile technology could produce fabrics woven with gold and silver metallic threads which were not harsh to touch, resulting in an increased demand for metallic dress materials in gauze, chiffon and lamé.

FRANCE 20th century

Designer unknown

Detail from *Dance dress* c.1925

silk tulle, gelatin sequins, glass beads

Purchased 1977   D86-1977

The pure line of tubular dresses was achieved by binding the breasts down flat. Short bobbed hair and cloche hats reflect the visual qualities of the New Modernist styles and machine age. The vogue for dances like the Charleston and foxtrot produced dresses designed to show the effect of movement and light by using beads, sequins, loose panels, fringes and flounces. It is impossible to assign a designer to many of these luxurious garments as the original label was attached to the matching slip. These were often worn out or lost and the styles were very similar. However 'Made in France' labels were sewn to the actual dress because of import laws, so we always have the country of origin.

The short chemise dress represents a very brief moment in fashion history. By 1924 this straight, waistless dress reached just below the knees. This look was often referred to as the 'garçonne' after the title of the popular novel *La Garçonne* by Victor Marguerite (1922), which features an emancipated heroine.

The discovery of Tutankhamen's tomb in November 1922 created a vogue for Egyptian motifs and colours which influenced contemporary fashion trends. The black muslin *Dance dress* (c.1925) embroidered all over with royal blue and gold sequins shows a strong Eygptian influence. The deep sapphire blue combined with gold conjures up the image of the ornate gold mask and sarcophagus of the young king. The skirt flares from the hip in a series of godets (triangular panels) and is decorated with alternate sequins, in vertical lines on the skirt and in swirling curves on the bodice.

FRANCE 20th century
Designer unknown
Gold and blue dance dress c.1925
cotton muslin, gelatin sequins
Purchased 1974   D233-1974

The black tulle *Dance dress* (c.1925) is embroidered with silver and white round glass beads, pink and black sequins and bugle beads. This complicated pattern includes a fully beaded bodice with a spray of sequin flowers focusing on the hips and the skirt is a mass of lines of black sequins. Beaded dresses were decorated by skilled embroiderers using a tambour hook (like a crochet hook except with a sharp point). The background fabric is stretched on a frame, the tambour hook is used to make a chain stitch to attach the beads or sequins. The fabric is worked from the back side. The *Silver and white dance dress* (c.1925) is beaded overall with a sophisticated geometric pattern and displays the intricate craftsmanship of this decorative work. The reverse side reveals fine trails of chain stitch applied by a tambour hook, and running stitch has also been used in places to secure the delicate loops of bugle beads. A craze for silver started in the 1920s in preference to gold; dresses like this one and many of the accessories were adorned with every type of decoration in this hue.

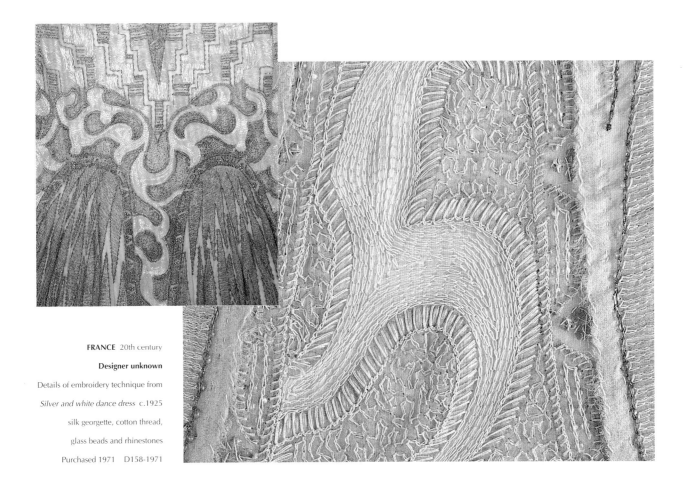

The technical simplicity of the chemise made it very easy to copy and it nearly destroyed the industry that created it. One Paris couturière, Madeleine Vionnet, stood apart. Her work was extremely difficult to copy as it was impossible for fashion journalists to describe. She is considered the greatest dressmaker of this century, revolutionising the cut and construction of womens clothes: 'with her scissors she changed fashion'. [1]

One must examine the anatomy of every customer. The dress must not hang on the body but follow its lines. It must accompany its wearer and when the woman smiles the dress must smile with her. The direction of the material, the weave and the crosslines on one hand; precision, cut, proportion on the other — that is what I oppose to the term fashion, which is an empty word and completely meaningless to a real dressmaker. [2]

Born in Aubervilliers, France in 1876, Vionnet was apprenticed to a local dressmaker when she was eleven. She went to England in 1896 and initially trained in London with the court dressmaker Kate O'Reilly. Returning to Paris in 1901, she spent a brief period as a sales assistant at Bechoff & David, then trained under the Callot sisters making toiles for Madame Gerber. In 1907 she joined the house of Doucet to revitalise their style. Vionnet was one of the first to abolish the use of corsets. She opened her own house in 1912, closing during the First World War and reopening in 1922.

VIONNET, Paris 1912–40

Madeleine Vionnet, designer 1876–1975

Evening dress c.1923

silk tulle, metallic threads, silk and metallic thread lamé

Purchased by The Art Foundation

of Victoria 1979   D20-1979

ELLIOT & WADE, London

Evening shoes c.1920

kid, paste buckle, elastic

Purchased 1974   D363-1974

Vionnet revolutionised the construction of fashion by cutting fabric on the cross or bias, which allowed for the optimum use of drape. The bias cut had previously been commonly used for collars, cuffs and trimmings but not for entire garments. Vionnet did not sketch her designs, she worked with the fabric directly on to a wooden figure about three feet high (just under one metre), with articulated joints. Draping the fabric and working in the round, she rarely used printed fabrics or decorative trims; the only interruption to the drapery and intricate cut were beading and embroidery, which never obscured the structure or shape of the dress.

Vionnet worked closely with fabric manufacturers, persuading them to create her favourite supple fabrics in two-metre widths. Her collections never attracted hordes of buyers because her garments were difficult to reproduce and copy. Albert Lesage executed the embroidery for Vionnet and had to develop a new type, which would not alter the fall of the fabric. He invented 'Luneville' (crochet embroidery); each stitch is worked to follow the warp or weft so as to not to go against the bias of the cloth.

The *Evening dress* (c.1923) in a rust silk tulle from the wardrobe of Lady Curzon, is embroidered entirely with a design of roses in shimmering metallic threads of gold, silver and bronze. This garment is a technical masterpiece, displaying a complicated structure and sophisticated detailing. The tulle dress has no fasteners, simply slipping over the head, like a typical 1920s shift. However, on close examination the dress reveals detailed pieces assembled like a complicated jigsaw. The dress has eight rows of roses graduating in size. The skirt section comprises five rows of scallop-shaped godets, each row consisting of nine godets, totalling forty-five individual tulle pieces. Each piece is cut on the bias, hand-embroidered with the abstract rose design and hand-sewn to the next piece by faggoting. The bodice is made from only four pieces of tulle, a basic front and back panel and two side gussets embroidered in the same floral design. This process of cutting up fabric and re-piecing it back together gave Vionnet her nickname of 'fashion's cubist'. The dress still has an attached tulle petticoat, and a separate gold slip. All the edges of the tulle are edged by a whip stitch, so that the main garment has no conventional straight seamline or hemlines. The result is that the dress appears to be made of one continuous piece and has an exceptionally full skirt.

The gold crepe lamé *Evening dress and underbodice* (c.1927) model no 22454, again from the wardrobe of Lady Curzon, features another sensational Vionnet technical innovation; a new type of collar using the drape of the fabric hanging forward in circular folds. Known as the 'Vionnet drip', it is now called the cowl. The full-length sleeveless dress has a dropped waistline, a double cowl neckline in the

VIONNET, Paris 1912–40

Madeleine Vionnet, designer 1876–1975

Evening dress and underbodice c.1927

silk and metallic thread lamé

Purchased by The Art Foundation

of Victoria 1979   D23AB-1979

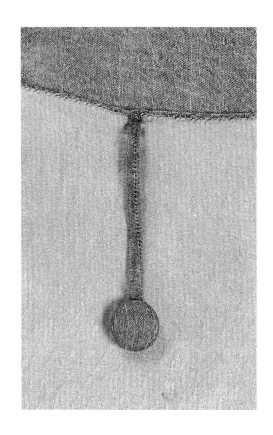

VIONNET, Paris 1912–40

Madeleine Vionnet, designer 1876–1975

Detail of inner construction of *Evening dress* c.1927

silk and metallic thread lamé, lead weight

Purchased by The Art Foundation

of Victoria 1979   D23A-1979

front and a single one in the back. The cowl is achieved by fabric cut on the bias with the addition of circular lead weights suspended on tabs from the inside of the bodice. The shape is also controlled by an inner waistband. The dress is cut from seven pieces of fabric machine-sewn together but hand-finished. The bodice cut on the bias, the skirt with the two centre-front and back panels cut on the straight and the side panels and corner sections cut on the cross, together culminate in a hem circumference of over four metres.

The dress has no fasteners. An underbodice of gold lamé ensures that the attractive décolletage of the cowl did not expose too much of the wearer's body. The inside of the bodice bears the original label, which reveals a lot about the high-quality work of this house. The label is embroidered in chain stitch, with the name 'Vionnet' in cream upon cream and on the end the designer's own thumb print dipped in black ink; the model number '22454' is stamped on the back.

By the 1930s Vionnet's style of fashion had changed but she still followed her basic principles of bias cut and shape. She also worked with wool and gabardine. During the 1930s, when built-up shoulders became the fashion, she produced her own version of this style by clever use of drapery rather than shoulder pads.

The *Day coat* (c.1938) is of fine black wool with a large black velvet stand-up collar and wrap-over lapel. It

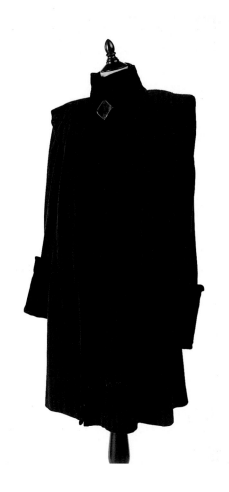

VIONNET, Paris 1912-40

Madeleine Vionnet, designer 1876–1975

Day coat c.1938

wool, silk velvet, metal, enamel

Purchased 1982   CT185-1982

fastens at the collar with one large green square enamel button. The coat is severe in line with accentuated collar and shoulders. The bulk on the shoulder line is created by a front panel which continues to form the back of the sleeve and the front of the sleeve is in one with the back panel. The garment is completed with two side panels. The coat bears the new 1930s Vionnet label with her red logo on cream satin depicting a woman in a simple dress standing on top of a column. Vionnet closed her house in 1939. After her lease ran out she had problems with her backer and decided to retire.

Gabrielle Bonheur Chanel was born in Saumur, France in 1883. Brought up in an orphanage, she began work as an assistant in a tailor's shop. She turned to millinery, and this led to her opening a hat shop financed by her boyfriend Arthur Capel. In 1914 she opened a dress shop on the rue Cambon, which closed during the First World War. Reopening as a couture salon in 1919, she quickly became one of the top designers of this century.

Chanel created simple, functional clothes that were easy and comfortable to wear. She believed that a women should,

be a caterpillar by day and butterfly at night. There is nothing more comfortable than a caterpillar and nothing more made for love than a butterfly. We need dresses that crawl and dresses that fly. [3]

In the early 1920s Chanel established black as a fashionable colour; throughout the nineteenth century it had been used exclusively for mourning dress and male costume. Chanel made the little black dress an indispensible part of any wardrobe.

Women think of all colours except the absence of colour. I have already said that black has it all. White too. Their beauty is absolute. It is the perfect harmony. [4]

Chanel changed the philosophy of clothing design by producing practical, simple styles that were comfortable to wear and looked fabulous.

The *Evening coat* (c.1930) in black silk panne velvet is beautifully shaped by shirring on the shoulders and cuffs. The long full raglan sleeves are gathered at the cuffs and lined with oyster silk satin. The coat would be worn with an ankle-length evening dress. The neck lining bears the understated house label which reflects so beautifully her design philosophies, a silk satin ribbon printed with 'Chanel' and no accompanying information. In 1939 Chanel closed her couture house, and retired to Switzerland. However, perhaps in response to Dior's exaggerated fashion creations, and to boost her perfume sales, she came out of retirement in 1954. Once again she produced wearable clothes until her death in 1971.

The couturière Jeanne Lanvin also began her design career as a milliner, on the rue du Faubourg-St-Honoré. By 1909 her business had developed into a full couture house. She specialised in creating matching garments for mother and daughter, and exquisitely crafted items.

The *Evening jacket* (summer 1929) of black chiffon features a striking geometric pattern in white glass bugle beads with an unusual collar formed like a necklace and decorated with mint-green glass bugle beads. The sleeve treatment is quite innovative with the sleeves gathered at the elbow.

The silk georgette *Evening dress* with matching shoulder *cape* (1930) in a rust-red floral pattern slips simply over the head and is worn over a vibrant red silk shift. The sleeveless dress with a V neckline is also shaped by gathering at the side seams from the waist to the hips, defining their outline and creating soft folds of drapery. The full skirt, made from six bias-cut godets, flares from the hips. The fluid lines of the dress are complemented by the asymmetrical short cape with its rounded edges. The cape simply ties

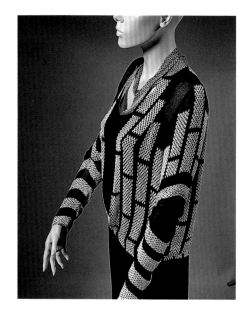

LANVIN, Paris est. 1909

Jeanne Lanvin, designer 1867–1946

Evening jacket summer 1929

silk crêpe, silk georgette, glass beads

Presented by Mrs A. Wilson 1982

CT12A-1982

CHANEL, Paris est. 1914

Gabrielle 'Coco' Chanel, designer 1883–1971

Detail from *Evening coat* c.1930

silk panne velvet, silk satin

Purchased 1974   D511-1974

at one shoulder, giving an impression of short sleeves. This clinging style of evening dress, with no ornamental detailing, was very revealing and required a perfect figure. The lines of the dress were easily distorted by bulges, so only the minimum amount of underwear could be worn. This was not an easy fashion to follow.

The 1930s saw a return to a more feminine style of fashion, with skirts between mid-calf and ankle length, made from flimsy fabrics. One of the leading designers was Edward Molyneux. In the spirit of Worth, this Englishman conquered fashionable Paris. Born in London in 1891, he trained under the local fashion house Lucille and served as a captain in the British Army during the First World War. In 1919 he

LANVIN, Paris est. 1909

Jeanne Lanvin, designer 1867–1946

Evening dress and cape spring-summer 1930

silk georgette, silk crêpe de Chine

Purchased 1977   D50ABC-1977

MOLYNEUX, London 1932–40

Captain Edward Molyneux, designer 1891–1974

Garden party dress c.1932

silk georgette

Purchased 1974   D25AB-1974

opened a couture house in Paris and was a leading fashion arbiter for several decades. In 1932 he opened a branch at 60 Grosvenor Square, London. Molyneux had a small clientele who loved the simple elegance of his clothes. He created practical day wear and stunning evening wear for the 'new' woman who travelled and led an active life style and needed light, simple but beautiful clothes.

The *Garden party dress* (c.1932) is sleeveless and mid-calf length in a silk chiffon featuring a delicate pattern of poppies in red, purple, green and mauve on a flesh-coloured ground. The dress shows the subtle detailing and finish which was an important feature of his work. It is shaped by smocking on the shoulders and at the apex of the godets around the hip section. The skirt is made up of floating panels of chiffon forming a handkerchief hemline of seven separate pieces. The underskirt in the same fabric is finished with a scalloped hem with a rolled edge. The original slip of flesh-coloured silk fastens on the side with sixteen hooks and embroidered loops and has his London label.

The Spanish-born Cristobal Balenciaga established his couture house in Paris in 1937. He was to dominate world fashion until his retirement in 1968. Balenciaga had extraordinary tailoring skills. He was able to make his own clothes from cutting to finishing, and to transform fabrics into strong sculptural shapes that combined with comfort revolutionised fashion trends.

The *'Infanta' gown* (1939) is a full-length evening dress of ivory duchess satin trimmed with parrot-green velvet. The bodice has short sleeves exaggerated at the shoulders by gathering and shoulder pads. Green velvet appliqué work in a scroll design outlines the neckline, centre front and waist of the bodice. The skirt is heavily gathered at the dropped waistline, emphasising the hip, and has a slight train at the back.

BALENCIAGA, Paris est. 1937

Cristobal Balenciaga, designer 1895–1972

'Infanta' gown 1939

duchess silk satin, silk velvet

Presented by Sarah Bostock 1993

CT1-1993

The shape and regal splendour of this dress were inspired by the work of the Spanish seventeenth-century court painter Diego Velazquez. His portraits of members of the royal court show the ornate costumes of the time, in particular his depictions of the infanta (the oldest daughter of the king and queen) wearing dresses with tight-fitting bodices and very wide skirts supported by hoop petticoats.

The gown fastens down the centre front with a zipper. This was a relatively new fastening device for women's fashion garments. It was originally devised for men's boots; the Italian-French designer Elsa Schiaparelli first used it for high-fashion garments in 1933. The zipper gave women an easy way to undo their clothes instead of the difficult back fasteners which relied on the services of a maid.

The original label from Balenciaga's couture house in Paris is stamped with the exclusive couture number 'No. 5045'. There are only two other known examples of this dress, one at the Costume Institute in New York and the other unfinished version at the Balenciaga Archives in Paris.

Notes

1   Cecil Beaton, *The Glass of Fashion*, Cassel, London, fascimile edition, 1989, p. 183.

2   Francis Kennett, *Secrets of the Couturiers*, Orbis, London, 1984, p. 39.

3   Jean Leymarie, *Chanel*, Rizzoli, New York, 1987, p. 167.

4   Ibid., p. 122.

The New Look

Christian Dior is probably the best-known name in the history of fashion. During a relatively short career of only ten years, he steered the major style directions of female clothing. Dior began his fashion career late in life. Born in 1905 in Normandy, France he first studied political science, and ran a commercial art gallery. In the 1930s he started selling fashion sketches to various Parisian couturiers, and later worked for Lucien Lelong from 1941 to 1946. In 1946 he persuaded the industrialist Marcel Boussac to provide the financial backing to open a couture house. In the spring of 1947 Dior's first collection caused a major revolution in dress. The 'Corolle' line, nicknamed the 'New Look' by fashion journalists, created a startling new fashion silhouette with rounded shoulders, corsetted wasp waists, padded hips, billowing longer skirts and the use of metres and metres of then still-rationed fabric. The romantic and feminine look was instantly popular after the austerity of the war years. In stark contrast to uniforms and basic utility dresses, Dior 'designed clothes for flower-like women, with rounded shoulders, full-feminine busts, and hand-span waists above enormous spreading skirts.' [1]

The strapless waltz-length (mid-calf) *Evening dress* (autumn-winter 1956), model number 83093, of beige silk tulle, is embroidered overall with silver and gold metallic threads and gold and silver sequins. The dress was worn with a gold lamé pleated cummerbund. The gold sequins form diamond shapes, graduating in size from small to large on panels that flow from bodice to hem. The fabric was specially made for this particular dress, resulting in the perfect orchestration and proportions of the pattern. The optical effects of the embroidery are stunning, including minute silver sequins randomly sewn across the surface to pick up an extra glimmer of light. The fabric was hand-embroidered and took hundreds of hours to make, costing thousands of dollars.

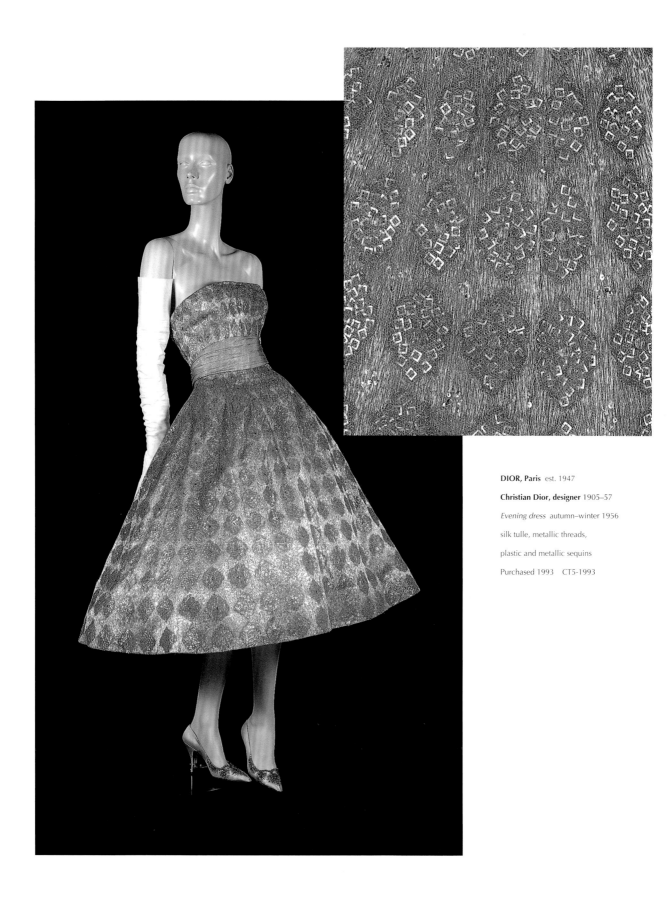

DIOR, Paris est. 1947

Christian Dior, designer 1905–57

Evening dress autumn–winter 1956

silk tulle, metallic threads,

plastic and metallic sequins

Purchased 1993   CT5-1993

It is not sufficently understood that embroidery is still done by hand, as in the eighteenth century and takes a month to three weeks. A ball dress may be entirely covered with millions of paillettes or pearls, each one has to be put on separately. [2]

The most fascinating aspect of a Dior garment is its inner construction. Built inside is the corselet of white silk taffeta including a bra top with wire cups, and the body shaped with eleven bones. The corset extends just below the hips and fastens with fifteen hooks and eyes. The wearer would probably have needed some assistance to get in and out of this dress with all those tiny hooks but would have required no additional supports. The outer fabric is closed by a zip. Underneath the skirt there are five tulle petticoats. The first layer of tulle is simply shaped by four darts, the second layer is fully gathered and the third layer, set four centimetres down from the previous layer, is rolled into the next layer of tulle and this construction repeats for the last two petticoats. This complicated inner foundation controls the shape of the skirt. 'I wanted my dresses to be constructed like buildings, moulded to the curves of the female form, stylising its shape'. [3]

DIOR, Paris est. 1947
Christian Dior, designer 1905–57
Detail of inner construction from
Evening dress autumn–winter 1956
silk tulle, metallic threads,
plastic and metallic sequins
Purchased 1993   CT5-1993

The type of dressmaking techniques Dior used in many of his silhouettes, the 'New Look' in particular, relied on supports, foundations, and stiffened fabrics typical of late nineteenth-century garments. Dior had no sewing skills, and the beautiful sculptural shapes he drew were interpreted first in muslin toiles lined in tarlatan to hold their shape, then translated by his expert technicians. Often the inside of a Dior gown reveals clumsy constructions to create these extreme designs.

The 'New Look' was a return to glamour and idealised womanly beauty. After decades of designers eliminating complex undergarments and artificial shapes, Dior reconstructed women in flattering geometric curves. After the hardships of war this unpractical and old-fashioned approach to clothing was very appealing, and was adopted in varying degrees of extravagance world-wide. In his later collections during the 1950s he created other new looks, including his well known 'H', 'A' and 'Y' lines. Dior died suddenly in 1957 and Yves Saint Laurent became the chief designer of the house.

There were only a few British designers based in London who managed to compete against the well-established fashion centre in Paris; all the best talent was based there. Norman Hartnell, known as the principal designer to British royalty, is a very under-estimated couturier. After training with the court dressmaker Madame Desire, and the London fashion house Lucille, he opened his own establishment in London in 1923. Hartnell became famous for sumptuous evening gowns encrusted with jewels and

sequins. These are unadventurous compared with his early day wear, which displays superb English tailoring, with unusual and inventive combinations of fabric and texture often at the forefront. Hartnell faced stiff competition from the very individualistic designers based in Paris. In 1927 he showed one of his collections at the Hotel Plaza Athenée, but he remained based in London. The Wall Street crash of 1929 and the following years of the Depression again led to English women supporting their local designers. In 1935 Hartnell received his first commission from the royal family, the wedding of Lady Alice Montagu-Douglas-Scott to the Duke of Gloucester; the Princesses Elizabeth and Margaret were bridesmaids. In 1947 Hartnell designed the wedding dress for Princess Elizabeth. In 1977 he was knighted, and he died two years later.

The *Cocktail dress and coat* (c.1949) show Hartnell's adaptation of a new-look style dress with a small waist and fuller skirt. The dress has a guipure lace bodice and short sleeves edged with black velvet; the bodice is joined to a black velvet skirt from the hip bordered with two rows of lace. The black velvet coat with lapel collar and long sleeves fastens with five large velvet buttons down the front and is trimmed with black guipure lace on the collar, pockets and across the back waist. Hartnell's day-wear designs are much more restrained than his extravagant evening wear.

The House of Jacques Fath created witty, often flirtatious garments blending new colour combinations with bold styling such as plunging necklines, asymmetrical shapes and tight-fitting skirts. Opening his Parisian couture house in 1937, he provided an imaginative alternative to the fashions of the major houses of Dior and Balenciaga, attracting a younger clientele with his distinctive clothes.

The *Evening dress* (c.1948) has an exotic mix of colour, texture, shape and drapery. The bodice has a striking woven-silk novelty fabric of fine black velvet pin stripes and a woven geometric pattern in pink and lime-green juxtaposed against the skirt of smouldering green and pink shot silk shrouded in black tulle. The bodice has a deep V neckline with a centre-front zip fastener and three-quarter-length sleeves. It is trimmed with a heavy black silk braid. The skirt is fitting to the hipline and features a distinctive front peplum trimmed with a black velvet bow; the skirt then flares

FATH, Paris 1937-57

Jacques Fath, designer 1912–54

Evening dress c.1948

silk shot taffeta, silk tulle, silk velvet,

novelty ribbed silk

Purchased 1972   D57-1972

out with fabric cut on the cross. Unfortunately Fath died of leukemia in 1954 at the height of his brilliance as a designer.

The drapery of ancient Greek and Roman clothing as it is known from sculpture has been an inspiration for many designers. Jean Dimitre Verginie opened his couture house Jean Dessès in Paris in 1937 and worked there until 1960. He was famous for dresses of chiffon or mousseline de soie in soft colours. He worked directly onto a dressmaker's mannequin, creating intricate draped evening dresses, and forming patterns by twisting and plaiting the fabric.

The *Evening dress* (c.1954) made from pale pink chiffon over a foundation of silk taffeta has tightly gathered chiffon over a corselet bodice, with a deep, horizontally pleated waistband and gathered chiffon straps. The full-length skirt is softly draped, forming an apron-style front with a fall each side making a bouffant shape at the hemline with a kick frill around the edge. It was worn by Mrs Nigel Newton at a ball to commemorate the visit of Queen Elizabeth II to Melbourne in 1954.

DESSES, Paris 1937–60

Jean Dessès, designer 1904–70

Evening dress c.1954

silk chiffon, silk taffeta

Presented by Mr John Kenny 1986

CT44-1986

DE RAUCH, Paris 1928–73

Madeleine De Rauch, designer

Evening dress and jacket 1956

silk satin

Purchased 1972   D61AB-1972

Madeleine de Rauch had one of the smaller couture houses of Paris. Established in the 1920s it remained active until 1973. The black satin full-length *Evening dress* (c.1956) has broad straps trimmed with bows. One strap is stitched in place to be worn off the shoulder. The sculptural qualities of this dress are evident, it has a fitted bodice, set into a natural waistline. The flared skirt is accentuated at the back with slightly more fullness from the hips. The controlled shape of this garment is also helped by the built-in corset and the support of three petticoats attached to the dress at the waist; the first is made from nylon, with a deep flounce of black tulle, and the top edge trimmed with a black satin ribbon bow. The second petticoat flares at the back from below the hips and is sewn with a panel of interfacing which acts like a very low bustle. The third petticoat is plain. The dress is worn with a contrasting evening jacket in white silk satin with short sleeves and no fasteners.

PIERRE BALMAIN, Paris est. 1946

Pierre Balmain, designer 1914–82

Day dress and apron 1955

silk velvet, wool jersey

Purchased 1972   D62AB-1972

Pierre Balmain initially studied architecture before embarking on a fashion career. In 1934 he worked for Molyneux and later Lelong, and opened his own house in 1946. He believed that 'dressmaking is the architecture of movement'. He was a leading influence during the 1950s, producing garments that appealed to older women. The *Day dress and apron* (1955) of dark brown velvet fastens elegantly down the back with self-covered buttons. It is worn with a wrap of brown wool jersey tied around the waist and trimmed with coarse fringing, providing an interesting juxtaposition of texture and shape.

By the 1960s the over-riding influence of exclusive couture and fashion on Western female dress was over and Paris also lost its monopoly on world trends. In 1960 a group of eleven couturiers formed a new association and began to show their prêt-à-porter (ready-to-wear) collections two weeks before the couture collections. Less expensive garments made in standard sizes and sold off the rack were taking over and designers were catering through boutiques and the better department stores for a wider, much less wealthy and younger market. In 1963 a group emerged who only made ready-to-wear clothing, they included designers such as Karl Lagerfeld and Emmanuelle Kahn.

Notes

1   *Dior by Dior*, trans. Antonia Fraser, Weidenfeld and Nicholson, London 1957, p. 25.

2   Ibid., p. 91.

3   Ibid., p. 25.

Fashion Essentials

The great couture houses from Worth to Dior nurtured and encouraged associated industries that produced fashion accessories ranging from the small details, such as feather fans, silk stockings, hat pins, coin purses, brassières and nylon stockings, to the indispensible and dominant focus areas of hats and shoes. Like their modern counterparts, the great fashion houses themselves would often co-ordinate exclusive accessory ranges to complement their fashions. Sometimes these were designed independently.

The designers and makers of head-dresses and footwear are often overlooked as we study the major artists of fashionable dress. However, they play an important role in completing the overall look of an outfit, and should also be recognised and appreciated for creating significant works in their own right. Unfortunately, the accessory designer is not always acknowledged and sometimes biographical and documentation details are impossible to find. Who can recall the creator of the cloche hat or the stiletto heel? Here, rather than attempt a comprehensive survey of hat and shoe fashions of the couture period, we focus only on the aspects reflected in the gallery's collection and we examine these items for their aesthetic, historical and practical features.

Since the nineteenth century, 'milliner' has been the term used for someone who trims, makes and sells hats or any other covering for the head. Millinery is a labour-intensive and exacting profession, entailing fine stitching, shaping, wire-work, and creating delicate trims. It is interesting to note that many of the influential couturiers, including Coco Chanel and Jeanne Lanvin, began their careers as milliners.

A fashionable woman of the turn of the century required different types of garments for specific occasions, there was not simply a choice of day or evening wear. She needed visiting, walking, afternoon, motoring, dinner and evening gowns, all of which required appropriate accessories. Hats were

FRANCE Designer unknown

Cream hat c.1910

chip straw, ostrich feathers

Presented by Thomas Harrison 1980

D214-1980

MARGUERITE PARAF, Paris

Saxe-blue cloche 1925

grosgrain silk

Presented by Lady Vestey 1980

D216-1980

FRANCE Designer unknown

Evening hat c.1935

silk georgette, lamé, silk floss, silk cord

Purchased 1977   D94-1977

PISSOT & PAVEY, London

Black toque c.1938

felt, sequins

Presented by Thomas Harrison 1980

D223-1980

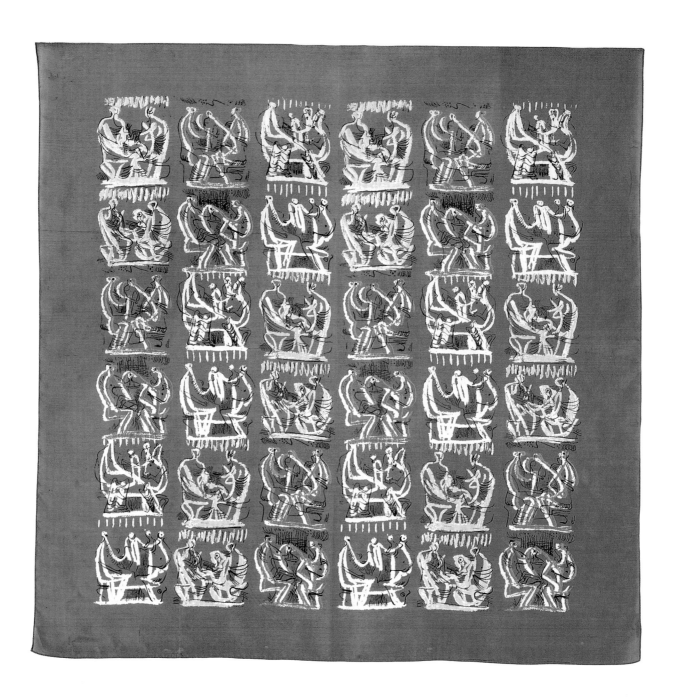

ASCHER LTD, London est. 1941

Henry Moore, designer 1898–1986

Family group scarf 1947

screenprint on silk

Purchased 1948   1904-17

compulsory habit for formal and informal occasions as a sign of respectability. A well-dressed woman could buy her hats ready-made or buy shapes and trimmings which her maid would make up.

Cecil Beaton fondly reminisces about his Aunt Jessie's extensive Edwardian wardrobe,

including the hat boxes — great square containers that held six hats apiece. In those days, mesh moulds were pinned on the sides, top and bottom of a bin so that the crown of a hat could be placed over the mould and fixed into place by a large hat pin piercing the mesh. In such manner, six hats could travel in a box without being crushed. And such headgear! Vast discs covered with funeral plumes of black ostrich feathers or white ospreys; hats for evening and hats for afternoon: hats for garden parties. [1]

Hats of the early twentieth century were large and extravagantly trimmed, for summer there were light straw hats smothered with flowers, lace, ribbons and feathers and in winter felt hats decorated in a sumptuous display of ribbons, feathers or imitation jewels.

The popular 'Merry Widow' style of hat originally created by the English design house Lucille for the famous London musical in 1907, promoted the fashion for large wide-brimmed hats elaborately trimmed with feathers. The *Cream hat* of chip straw (c.1910), with a flat brim swathed with ostrich feathers dyed in shades of pink and lilac, was worn slightly tilted.

Feathers were a common decoration. Active campaigns launched by philanthropic and conservationist movements worked to protect rare birds such as the grebe, heron and egret, which were threatened with extinction due to this fashion trend. In 1906 this led to Queen Alexandra forbidding the use of osprey plumage at court. Ostrich, which replaced it, was seen as a more appropriate trim as the ostrich birds had been farmed in South Africa since 1865 and it was believed that the feathers could be removed without hurting the bird. Hat pins were introduced at the end of the nineteenth century to secure the hat to the hairstyle and as a final decorative touch. Varying in length from thirteen to twenty-eight centimetres, the sharp end of the pin was shielded by a protective butt to prevent damage to passers by. Hats, however, became so large that they and their hat pins were a menace. They were not suitable for sportswear and smaller, boater styles were worn. For the new activity of motoring a large veil was wrapped around the hat to protect the wearer from dust and losing the hat in the wind.

By the 1920s there was a major change in the shape of hats. The new bobbed or shingled hair led to a tighter-fitting style which did not rely on a hat pin and a full hairstyle to fix it to the head. This type of hat, with a very narrow brim and crown fitting closely to the head like a helmet, was called a cloche and could only be worn with short hair. The *Saxe-blue cloche* of grosgrain silk (1925) created by Marguerite Paraf of Paris was originally worn by Dame Nellie Melba. The hat features vertical- and diagonal-pattern top stitching trimmed with a bow.

Short hairstyles from the shingle to the Eton crop dominated until 1929 when the fashions changed and ankle-length skirts were worn with longer, often curled hair. Smaller hats that sat on one side of the head

CHRISTIAN DIOR, Paris est. 1947

Cream hat c.1956

straw, artificial flowers

Purchased 1972   D59-1972

AAGE THARRUP, London est. 1932

Aage Tharrup, designer born 1908

White hat c.1948

felt

Presented by Miss V. Carrad 1968

1956-5

JEANNE LANVIN, Paris est. 1909

Parrot-green toque c.1955

felt, silk

Presented by Mrs S. M. Wauchope 1991

CT60-1991

were in vogue. Glamorous evening hats complemented the slinky lines of the new bias-cut clothes. The French *Evening hat* (c.1935) has a close-fitting crown, hand-embroidered with multicoloured flowers and green silk cord appliqué leaves on black georgette, the front is trimmed with a gold lamé bow.

The fashion silhouette of the mid 1930s with broad shoulders and a higher waist looked best worn with head-hugging hats often in abstract, sculptural shapes and sitting high on the head. A major influence on fashion in the 1930s was the Paris-based Elsa Schiaparelli, who collaborated with the major surrealist artist Salvador Dali and unleashed on the world a new type of fashion which juxtaposed unusual shapes, patterns and ideas in garments. During this decade she also created the 'shoe' hat and the 'lamb chop' hat, stylish fantasy designs. The *Black toque* (c.1938), designed by Pissot & Pavey of London, is moulded of felt with a very high crown shaped like a chignon. The hat is highlighted with two striking bands of shimmering black sequins and is typical of the eccentric shapes in fashion.

During the Second World War head scarves were worn as a practical alternative to expensive hats. This trend encouraged Zika Ascher, who with his wife Lida founded the firm Ascher Ltd in 1941 to commission important contemporary artists to design scarves. All the artists were asked to create a design for a square of thirty-six inches (ninety-one centimetres) in any medium and using as many colours as they wished. Any technical difficulties involved in translating the works to fabric were solved by Ascher. Initially, he commissioned British artists, such as Henry Moore, Ben Nicholson and Graham Sutherland; after the war he worked with major European artists including Henri Matisse and Andre Derain. The scarves were screen-printed by hand, and an enormous amount of experimentation was required to reproduce the texture and fine lines of the original works on a base of silk.

The scarf could be framed as a work of art or looked attractive when draped and worn as an accessory. This exciting project combined the latest developments in textile printing with contemporary art and fashion. Leading British sculptor Henry Moore developed a special and enduring relationship with Ascher. The scarves *Family group* and *Standing figures*, designed by Henry Moore in 1948, were taken directly from the artist's sketchbooks. The wax crayon and watercolour wash used in the original drawings was accurately translated and *Family group* was also developed into a repeat design. Ascher scarves were worn by fashionable women from the 1940s until the firm closed in the late 1980s.

After the Second World War the revival of hats as an important fashion accessory was due to Christian Dior. His 'New Look' silhouette launched large wide-brimmed hats to balance the width of the new fuller skirts.

The Danish-born milliner Aage Tharrup came to England in 1932 after a short stay in India, where he had designed hats for the rich English residents. His styles feature austere and inventive shapes. He designed the famous 'burnous drape' for the actress Marlene Dietrich, and in his memoirs he recalls, 'How was I to match her mysterious glamour? I got the idea of a bedouin's head-dress, and adapted it in amber and black tulle with a beaded band in bronze to keep it in place'. [2]

Tharrup was also milliner to the Queen Mother and Queen Elizabeth II. In 1947 he visited Melbourne and, 'at the elegant store Georges where I showed, everyone turned out for the opening night in full evening dress; laying one bogy for me. My cocktail hats would not be despised'. [3] The *White hat* of felt (c.1947) has a wide brim cut away at the back and a shallow crown. The hat is from the wardrobe of

Miss Reta Findlay, who was the director of the Melbourne department store Georges until 1958, and she possibly acquired it during the visit.

The *Black hat* (c.1947) by Otto Lucas of London, shaped like a large propeller wing of felt and swathed with net under the brim, represents this 'New Look' trend. Born in Germany in 1903, Lucas moved to London in 1932 to establish a hat salon. His hats were often featured in the movies of the 1940s and 1950s and the Duchess of Windsor was one of his well-known clients. He died tragically in a plane crash in 1971.

The large romantic *Cream hat* (c.1956) from the house of Christian Dior is of straw with a flat crown and a wide brim. It is elegantly decorated with a spray of two large water lilies, including buds and leaves, and shows similiarities with the large hats of the Edwardian period.

Jeanne Lanvin trained initially as a milliner before embarking on her very successful fashion career. After her death in 1946 her house continued to operate under various designers, including Antonio Castillo from 1950 to 1963. Like many other major couture houses Lanvin produced its own range of hats. The *Parrot-green toque* (c.1955), of felt shaped in the form of a cornucopia, is trimmed with black petersham ribbon around the edge and finished with a bow. This reflects an alternative trend to wide-brimmed hats, with smaller, more sculptural styles.

By the mid 1950s the importance of the hat was waning; no longer did a women have to cover her head. The art of coiffure took over with permanent waves, hairspray and large bouffant hairstyles putting the finishing touch to an outfit.

From the late nineteenth century until 1910 women's feet remained hidden under long garments, and one would have only seen glimpses of footwear as the wearer moved. The Victorian-style buttoned or laced boot was correct outdoor wear until 1920. Boots were often fastened with more than ten buttons and required the use of a button hook to fasten the boots without bending down.

The Parisian firm Pinet, a contemporary of Worth, inscribed its label with 'Exposition Universale de Paris 1867', the international exhibition where the firm proudly displayed its wares and high-quality techniques. The intricate and hand-crafted boots by Pinet reflect the extravagant materials in use. The *Lady's pink boot* (c.1880) with a slightly pointed toe and a Louis-style heel (named after shoes worn by the French eighteenth-century court of Louis XIV) is in pink corded silk embroidered with yellow silk floss in a floral decoration and has a scalloped edge fastened with ten 22-carat gold shank buttons. Another boot from Pinet in navy-blue satin is richly hand-embroidered with chenille ribbon and silk thread in moss-green, scarlet, pale blue, pink and cream in a delicate pattern of rose buds and leaves and is fastened by front lacing. A third example incorporates a brocade background in cream, browns and blue depicting vine leaves and grapes and also features ten 22-carat gold shank buttons. Dress boots were worn for special occasions.

By 1920 the shoe was completely visible and became a very noticeable and dominant feature of fashionable dress. The *Evening shoe* (c.1920) by Elliot & Wade of London is made of gold and silver kid and uses elastic in its construction. The high vamp is decorated with appliqué of gold kid and a paste buckle disguises an elastic insert, which helped in putting on the shoe. Elastomeric fibres had been in use since the late nineteenth century. Unfortunately, the cotton fabric woven with threads of rubber perished

PINET, Paris

Black evening shoe c.1926

leather, silk, silk thread

Presented by Mrs John Allen 1985

CT50-1985

PINET, Paris

Evening shoe c.1926

silk satin, kid

Presented by Mrs Gwen Fisher 1985

CT27-1985

BELGIUM
Designer unknown

Black and gold evening shoe c.1925

silk satin, kid, glass button

Presented by Miss Nina Bagot 1972

D97-1972

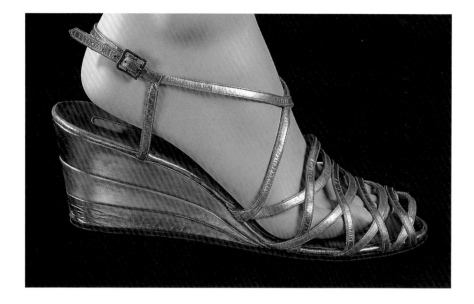

FERRAGAMO, Florence est. 1927

Salvatore Ferragamo, designer 1898–1960

Evening 'wedgie' sandal 1948

kid, cork

Presented by Miss V. Carrad 1968

1957-5

easily under strain. During the 1920s some exciting styles and decorative treatments developed. High heels dominated, from the curvy Louis XIV-style high heel to the Cuban, and essential shapes included the pointed shoe with high heel and single-bar strap, T-bar and cutaway. The *Black Evening shoe* (c.1926) by Pinet of Paris has a T-bar fastening edged with silver kid piping, the vamp is hand-embroidered with multicoloured silk flowers.

Shoes of the 1920s were worn with 'artificial silk' stockings. Artificial silk, or rayon, discovered by Courtauld in the early 1900s, revolutionised stockings. By 1920 it replaced the wool and silk previously used, which were heavy, expensive and uncomfortable. The flapper leg was always covered with brightly coloured stockings to complement the shoes.

The Belgian *Black and gold evening shoe* (c.1925) is made with a black satin ground decorated overall with cut work of gold kid appliqué in circular bands creating a pulsating optical effect. These bold geometric patterns dominated after the Paris Exhibition of Decorative Arts in 1925, which launched the Art Deco style. Subtler effects using fabric or pearlised leather in soft colours were popular by 1930. The *Brocade evening shoe* (c.1930) by Bally of Switzerland is covered with an exclusively designed fabric in the delicate, glowing shades of pink, yellow, and turquoise shot with gold metal threads in a striking geometric pattern. The vamp is edged with gold kid and a stylised bow is appliquéd on the right side.

Shoes of the 1930s, were simpler and cut higher. Comfort became an essential design consideration. Sandals were very popular for casual and special occasions. Floating dresses of chiffon required strappy open evening sandals. The *Evening sandal* (c.1935) of yellow, red and black printed silk is shot with a pattern of silver metallic thread. The vamp with open work is decorated with straps of gold and silver plaited leather.

Known as the 'Shoemaker of Dreams' Salvatore Ferragamo revolutionised the design of women's shoes. 'There is no limit to beauty, no saturation point in design, no end to the materials a shoemaker may use to decorate his creations so that every woman may be shod like a princess and a princess may be shod like a fairy queen'.[4] Born in Bonito, Italy in 1898, Ferragamo was apprenticed at a young age to the village cobbler, and became a successful craftsman. In 1923 he emigrated to the United States, studied shoe and production methods, and created period-costume shoes for the movies. He also opened an exclusive shoe boutique in Hollywood, making shoes for such clients in the film industry as Gloria Swanson.

Ferragamo returned to Italy in 1927 and made Florence his base. Combining successfully inventive design with high-quality production skills, he created shoes in shapes that allowed the foot to flex. Instead of using a leather arch support, he inserted a thin piece of steel into the sole. He designed shoes that were both comfortable and beautiful to look at.

In 1936, the shortage of top-grade light tensile steel used in the shank of his shoes led Ferragamo to experiment with cork. By filling in the space between the heel and the ball of the foot, he invented the wedge heel. At first 'some raved at the wedgies' style and beauty, some said they were dreadful and looked like orthopaedic shoes,[5] but they became one of his most popular styles.

The *Evening 'wedgie' sandal* (c.1948) in gold and silver kid is a timeless and significant example of the advanced styling of Ferragamo. The wedge heel is formed of three layers of cork covered with strips of gold and silver kid. The upper is formed with thin strips of silver and gold kid with a sling back.

Ferragamo was important in elevating the status of the shoe designer and maker as an independent source of style in the fashion world rather than just following the dictates of the Parisian couturiers. Known for using inventive materials such as cellophane and perspex, he also created the infamous platform sole.

One of the most deadly shoe fashions of the century was the stiletto. First seen in the Dior collections, this style was originally created by the French designer Roger Vivier. Vivier had his own firm after 1932, and in 1953 he became shoemaker to Dior. The stiletto had a very narrow heel, and the sharp end caused an enormous amount of damage to floor coverings. Aesthetically, the shoe created the image of a fragile woman delicately supported on little more than air.

Long, fine, pointed toes were called needles. The emerald-green *Satin evening shoe* (c.1956) with a triple needle toe and stiletto heel was created by the Italian firm Pancaldi and shows the extremes of this extravagant styling.

The stiletto heel was still worn in 1960, but in a lower and more refined form. Alternatives to the narrow heels were flat shoes or broad-heel pumps popular with younger women and worn with denim jeans. By 1960 the extreme changes produced by haute couture designers each season had lost ground, which heralded in a time of flexible styling in shoes ranging from fun to functional.

N o t e s

1   Cecil Beaton, *The Glass of Fashion*, Cassell, London, 1989, p. 23.

2   Aage Tharrup, *Heads & Tales*, Cassell, London, 1956, p. 66.

3   Ibid., p. 199.

4   Salvatore Ferragamo, *Shoemaker of Dreams*, Harrap, London, 1957, p. 214.

5   Ibid., p. 145.

Dior and Beyond

The death of Christian Dior in 1957 marks the end of a century of domination by haute couture over Western fashion. Dior, with his incredible flair for publicity, brought fashion to its highest level of international acclaim. The 'New Look', for instance, became the principal style copied by retailers world-wide. Dior's promotion and marketing techniques gave his collections huge exposure and notoriety, and widespread influence. The world looked to Paris for new directions in clothing design and the major couture houses controlled the silhouette, from the length of the hem to the width of the skirt and even the shades of colour used in fabrics. Paris was the supreme centre of world fashion. But by the late 1950s the nature and sources of style began to change.

Dress began to loose its formality. For example, gloves and hats were no longer compulsory habit and conventions for day and evening wear were less distinct. A new generation of women emerged, who no longer were attracted to the allure of a couture garment with its countless fittings and expensive price tag. Ready-to-wear clothes in standard sizes and styles that could be purchased in one visit to a boutique took over. A revolution occurred in social values that changed fashion for- ever, especially the influence of feminism, the needs of career women and the use of the contraceptive pill. The authority of high fashion and its compulsive attraction began to waver.

Yves Saint Laurent became chief designer at the House of Dior after Dior's sudden death. The first major sign of social changes reflected in fashion occurred with his 'Beat' collection of 1960, featuring turtle-neck sweaters and leather trousers, which at first was labelled a disaster but which appealed to younger women. By 1960, the effects of the post-war baby boom had seen a marked increase in the size of the population under twenty-five, and the need arose for clothing that catered for this age group and its more relaxed life style.

Designers catered for the new youth market. London-based Mary Quant created mini skirts (a major contrast to the mid-calf skirts of the 1950s), while in Paris Pierre Cardin produced unisex body suits and Andre Courrèges the space-age look. During the 1960s alternative fashions developed challenging new clothing concepts, including disposable paper dresses and garments made from metal or plastic, which presented the notion of 'anti-fashion'. Young people were tired of traditional clothing images and Yves Saint Laurent, now in control of his own house, produced garments inspired by pop art and even motor-cycle gangs. He recognised social changes and the demise of the absolute fashion edict, claiming 'Now that women have liberated themselves from our dictatorship and the corset of other people's ideas, they themselves become more important than the clothes they wear'. [1]

These new fashion trends came from a diversity of sources, with major artists working in the new fashion centres of New York, London and Milan as well as in Paris, and were inspired by the world of popular music and street wear. Today, haute couture still survives with its small client base, but it no longer exclusively steers fashion or is the sole source of new ideas or artists. The leaders of style are from all levels of fashion and cover the globe.

The years from Worth to Dior saw phenomenal changes. Fashion artists were legitimised and recognised as a creative force; major advances were made in the practical function of women's clothing and in the development of modern aesthetic ideas; new construction techniques and major discoveries in textile technologies were made. However the creative influences of the great couturiers from this period are still with us, from the label on our dress to the presentation of garments on live mannequins and in the invention of certain clothing types. The costumes on display in this exhibition represent the clothing innovations of the past, provide us with inspiration, and celebrate the arts of fashion design and of fine dressmaking techniques.

N o t e

1   Axel Madsen, *Living for Design: The Yves Saint Laurent Story*, Delacarte Press, New York, 1979, pp. 29–30.

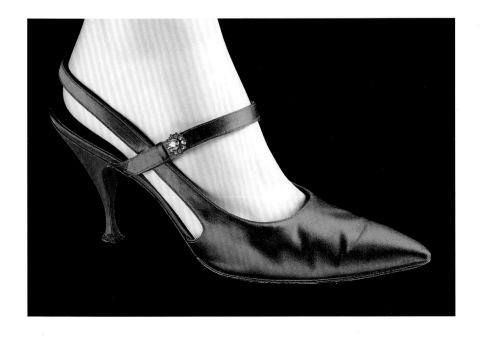

PANCALDI, Bologna

Satin evening shoe c.1956

silk satin, leather, metal

Presented by Mrs Aubrey Gibson 1981

CT23-1981

Select Bibliography

Adburgham, Alison, *Shops and Shopping 1800–1914*, George Allen and Unwin, London, 1967.

Arnold, Janet, *Patterns of Fashion 2*, Drama Book Publishers, New York, new edition, reprint 1991.

Battersby, Martin, *The Decorative Twenties*, Studio Vista, London, 1969.

Beaton, Cecil, *Fashion*, Victoria & Albert Museum, London, 1971.

Bradfield, Nancy, *Costume in Detail 1730–1930*, George G. Harrap, London, 1968.

Carter, Ernestine, *The Magic of Names of Fashion*, Weidenfeld and Nicolson, London, 1980.

Clark, Rowena (ed.), *Fabulous Fashion 1907–67*, International Cultural Corporation of Australia, Melbourne, 1981.

Coleman, Elizabeth Ann, *The Opulent Era: Fashions of Worth, Doucet and Pingat*, Brooklyn Museum, Thames and Hudson, London, 1989.

de Marly, Diana, *Worth Father of Haute Couture*, Camelot Press, London, 1980.

de Osma, Guillermo, *Mariano Fortuny: His Life and Work*, Aurum Press, London, 1980.

de Teliga, Jane, 'Twentieth century costume: A focus for Australian Art Museums', *Art and Australia*, Fine Arts Press Pty Ltd, Sydney, 1981.

Dior by Dior, trans. Antonia Fraser, Weidenfeld and Nicolson, London, 1957.

Dorner, Jane, *Fashion in the Forties & Fifties*, Ian Allen Ltd, Surrey, 1975.

Drusedow, Jean L., 'In Style: Celebrating Fifty Years of the Costume Institute', *The Metropolitan Museum of Art Bulletin*, Fall, vol. xiv, no. 2, New York, 1987.

Fashion 1900–1939, The Scottish Arts Council and The Victoria & Albert Museum, 1975.

Fortuny, Fashion Institute of Technology, New York, 1981.

Ginsburg, Madeleine et al., *Four Hundred Years of Fashion*, Victoria & Albert Museum, London, 1984.

Ginsburg, Madeleine, *The Hat*, Studio Editions, London, 1990.

Glynn, Prudence, *In Fashion: Dress in the Twentieth Century*, Oxford University Press, New York, 1978.

Gutsche, Thelma, *No Ordinary Woman; the Life and Times of Florence Phillips*, Howard Timmins, Cape Town, 1966.

Jouve, Marie-Andree and Demornex, Jacqueline, *Balenciaga*, Rizzoli International Publications, New York, 1989.

Kennett, Frances, *Secrets of the Couturiers*, Orbis, London, 1984.

Liberty's 1875–1975, Victoria & Albert Museum, London, 1991.

Lynam, Ruth (ed.), *Couture*, Doubleday & Co, New York, 1972.

Martin, Richard and Koda Harold, *Flair*, Rizzoli International Publications, New York, 1992.

Mendes, Valerie and Hinchcliffe, Frances M., *Ascher*, Victoria & Albert Museum, London, 1987.

Mendes, Valerie et al., *Salvatore Ferragamo: The Art of the Shoe 1927–1960*, Centro Di della Edifimi srl, Florence, 1987.

McDowell, Colin, *McDowell's Directory of Twentieth Century Fashion*, Frederick Muller, London, 1984.

Milbank, Caroline Rennolds, *Couture*, Thames and Hudson, London, 1985.

Newton, Stella Mary, *Health, Art & Reason*, Fakenham and Reading, London, 1974.

Norman Hartnell, Art Gallery and Museums Brighton, St Edmondsbury Press, Suffolk, 1985.

Robinson, Julian, *The Golden Age of Style*, Orbis, London, 1976.

Tarrant, Naomi, *Haute Couture at Spink*, Spink & Son, London, 1989

The Marchioness Curzon of Kedleston, *Reminiscences*, Hutchinson and Co, London, 1955.

Wilcox, Claire and Mendes, Valerie, *Modern Fashion in Detail*, Victoria & Albert Museum, London, 1991.